THE LOST PROPHET

THE LOST PROPHET

The Book of Enoch
and its influence on Christianity

MARGARET BARKER

Before these things Enoch was hidden,
and no one of the children of men knew where he was hidden,
and where he abode, and what had become of him.

(1 Enoch 12.1)

ABINGDON PRESS
Nashville

THE LOST PROPHET

Copyright © Margaret Barker 1988

This book is printed on acid-free paper.

Library of Congress Cataloging-in-Publication Data

BARKER, MARGARET, 1944-
   The lost prophet.

   "First published in Great Britain, 1988, SPCK"—T.p. verso.
Includes index.
   1. Ethiopic book of Enoch—Criticism, interpretation, etc. I.
Title.
BS1830.E7B37   1989   229'.913   88-35121
ISBN 0-687-22779-8 (alk. paper)

First published in Great Britain 1988
SPCK
Holy Trinity Church, Marylebone Road, London NW1 4DU

Abingdon Press edition published 1989

MANUFACTURED IN THE UNITED STATES OF AMERICA

Contents

In Memory of
Roger Cowley
who died on 5 April 1988

The Prophet

With fainting soul athirst for Grace,
I wandered in a desert place
And at the crossing of the ways
I saw the sixfold seraph blaze;
He touched mine eyes with fingers light
As sleep that cometh in the night:
And like a frightened eagle's eyes,
They opened wide with prophecies.
He touched mine ears, and they were drowned
With tumult and a roaring sound:
I heard convulsion in the sky,
And flights of angel hosts on high,
And beasts that move beneath the sea,
And the sap creeping in the tree.
And bending to my mouth he wrung
From out of it my sinful tongue,
And all its lies and idle rust,
And twixt my lips a-perishing
A subtle serpent's forked sting
With right hand wet with blood he thrust.
And with his sword my breast he cleft
My quaking heart thereout he reft,
And in the yawning of my breast
A coal of living fire he pressed.
Then in the desert I lay dead,
And God called unto me and said:
'Arise, and let my voice be heard,
Charged with my will go forth and span
The land and sea, and let my word
Lay waste with fire the heart of man.'

A. S. Pushkin
tr. Maurice Baring in
Have You Anything to Declare? (Heinemann 1936)

Note: Non-Biblical Books

This is a short but inaccurate title to describe the less well-known texts mentioned in this book. Several of the texts mentioned below are, or have been, biblical. Some are now classed as apocryphal, or deutero-canonical. Others are pseudepigraphical, and can be read in any of the collections of texts listed on p. 15.

The Odes of Solomon (not to be confused with the Psalms of Solomon) is an early Christian hymnbook from the end of the first century. The Odes have many Jewish features (as does Christianity!), and it is not certain whether they were originally Jewish or Christian. The most complete version has survived in Syriac, but there are some in Coptic and one in Greek.

The Ascension of Isaiah is another text of unknown origin which probably had a Jewish core and was expanded by Christian writers. It tells of the martyrdom of Isaiah in the time of the evil king Manasseh (2 Kings 21.1–18) and of his visionary ascent through seven heavens to the great throne of God. The book gives a valuable picture of Christian belief at the end of the first century; it has survived complete in Ethiopic, and in fragments in Greek, Latin, Coptic and Old Slavonic.

Jubilees is a rewriting of Genesis, and takes its name from the author's way of reckoning time in Jubilees, periods of forty-nine years. He writes to show that the Law of Moses was observed even before the time of Moses, and that the patriarchs kept even the later, non-biblical expansions of the Jewish Law. It survives in Ethiopic, and there are Latin fragments. Several manuscripts in fragment form have also been found at Qumran, suggesting a date in the early or middle second century BC.

The Testaments of the Twelve Patriarchs are the 'death-bed' speeches of each of Jacob's twelve sons, the patriarchs of the tribes of Israel. They warn their descendants of future evils, and exhort them to an upright life. They comprise probably a Jewish work which has been adapted by a Christian writer. Fragments of similar texts have been found in Aramaic at Qumran, but the Testaments of the Twelve Patriarchs have survived only in Greek, with versions in Armenian and Old Slavonic.

The Genesis Apocryphon is another rewriting of Genesis, of which fragments have been found at Qumran. The writer involves far more angelic creatures in his story than does the writer of the biblical Genesis.

2 Esdras is a book with many names. It is also called 4 Ezra, 4 Esdras, and, in the Slavonic Bible, 3 Esdras. It can be found in the Apocrypha. The book describes seven visions of Ezra dated thirty years after the fall of Jerusalem in 586 BC, but in fact refers to the situation after the fall of Jerusalem to the Romans in AD 70. The book explores the problem of evil, and shows the questions being asked after the great disaster. It was probably written in Hebrew, but survives only in other languages: Latin, Syriac, Ethiopic, Arabic, Armenian, Sahidic and Georgian. It was a very popular work.

The Prayer of Manasseh. Most Greek versions of the Old Testament have an appendix to the Book of Psalms which is a collection of songs mostly drawn from Old Testament writings, e.g. the Song of Moses from Exodus 15. One of them is the Prayer of Manasseh, the repentance of the evil king who is supposed, among other things, to have murdered Isaiah. A prayer is mentioned in 2 Chronicles 33.18, but this prayer is probably a later composition inspired by the same story. It survives in Greek and Syriac and can be found in the Apocrypha.

2 Enoch, the Secrets of Enoch, was formerly in Greek, and possibly written in Alexandria. Its date is not known, but it could be fairly early, perhaps late first century, as it was used by other Christian writings. It describes the seer's ascent to the great throne. Sometimes it is called the Slavonic Enoch because it has survived only in Old Slavonic.

The Epistle of Barnabus is a Christian 'letter', in the manner of Paul's letters, from the early first century.

The Shepherd of Hermas is a series of revelations to Hermas by the Church, who appears as a woman, by the shepherd angel, and by the great angel. It was written in the early part of the first century, and for a while was included in the New Testament.

The Gospel of Thomas is a collection of sayings of Jesus. A Coptic translation was among the Gnostic books discovered in 1945 at Nag Hammadi in upper Egypt. Several fragments are also known in Greek. Much of this gospel appears to be very early Christian material, and resembles the sayings collection (Q) used as a source by Matthew and Luke. It is thought to have come from a second-generation community in Palestine or Syria, and thus to be as old as the New Testament Gospels.

Introduction

The Lost Prophet is Enoch; lost because for fifteen centuries the Western Churches have not had this ancient visionary book, even though the first Christians knew and used it. It was rediscovered two hundred years ago, and an English translation has been available for a century, yet still it is hardly known at all outside specialist circles. This is a pity, because the Book of Enoch has long been recognized as the most important Jewish writing from the New Testament period. It sheds great light on the beliefs and teachings of the early Church, and I have found it a source of inspiration for much of my own preaching.

When fragments of the Book of Enoch were found among the Dead Sea Scrolls, it was realized that this was a very ancient text. Although it was known and used by the first Christians, it was not written by them but was a part of their Jewish heritage. Exactly when and where the book (or rather 'books', because it is a collection of texts) originated is still debated, but there is the distinct possibility that it is as old as some of the Old Testament. All this is very fascinating for those with a specialist interest in the ancient world. But the real importance of Enoch does not lie in the fact that it is a 'lost' Jewish text preserved only by Christian hands. It lies in the questions raised by the book and the world-view it presents.

The events and developments of the twentieth century have raised new questions for thinking Christians for which the Bible as presently read seems to give little guidance. We have seen a massive increase in scientific knowledge, which has altered our way of living for better and for worse. We have seen the spirit of scientific inquiry pressing freely onwards, with one or two lone voices asking quaintly old-fashioned moral questions. We have developed a new awareness of our environment, and realized that we have been poisoning and destroying the creation through an exploitation of its resources. We have the Bomb and the potential to destroy everything. We have seen evil in wars and weapons that is beyond belief. We have seen the

I

growth of the mass media, and the power to shape opinion handed to those who are best presented, best packaged and best advertised.

Growing up among this tawdry debris there are new, green things: an awareness of our relationship to the earth which sustains us as mother, rather than obeys us as slave, and a groping towards the unspoken and unspeakable mysteries of life. Sometimes this latter has led to an interest in oriental religions, sometimes to the charismatic churches; both indicate the same need for the irrational and the beyond in an increasingly unsatisfactory world of precision-packed information. The circular shape of our liturgically reformed services has also been a mixed blessing; we now look across to each other, when what we need is to look up and beyond. The most significant development has been the change in the role and status of women. The full force of this wave has yet to break, and, when it does, the effect upon our churches, not only on their structures but also on their presentation of theology, will be devastating. For fifteen centuries at least, women have been the victims of the Adam and Eve story, and have been blamed for being the victims. All this will change.

How is an ancient visionary text relevant to all these things? It is not relevant, it must be said, in the sense that it is an ancient prediction of the twentieth century miraculously recovered midway through that century offering instant answers to all its questions. But it is very relevant in the sense that it offers insights, perspectives, models and myths (there are many fashionable words) which could not have been seen as relevant in a situation that did not ask certain questions. It is, I think, no accident that the recovery of the pre-Christian Enoch, and the revival of interest in these texts, has happened in the twentieth century.

Enoch is a strange book, and not at all easy to read. But when it begins to come into focus we can see astute observations about the potential dangers of scientific knowledge freed from moral restraint, about the consequences of destroying the natural harmonies of nature, and about the power of those who shape opinion and expectations. Enoch is based upon a theory of the origin of evil which does not involve Adam and Eve and original sin, and the massive burden of human guilt upon which the Churches have fed for so long. Enoch describes the corruption of superhuman forces which have oppressed and diminished the creation, and put it in bondage to decay. Humankind, men and women in their natural state, are victims to be rescued from this evil.

The greatest importance of Enoch is that it was not only a pre-Christian book, but also a post-Christian book, a text from their Jewish background kept and used by the earliest churches. These ideas about the nature of evil, the danger of corrupted skills and scientific knowledge, and the bonds of natural harmony in creation, must have been a part of the earliest Christians' world-view, a part of what they assumed. When we use Enoch as a 'context' for the New Testament, many early Christian ideas come into a much clearer focus, and many of the gaps in the New Testament can be bridged.

I have tried to make this ancient book available to the non-specialist reader. The world of scholarship is closed for many people, and the ancient languages form an insuperable barrier. Scholarship is often viewed with suspicion and felt to be destructive and irrelevant. The concerns of scholars are seen as remote from those who actually read and use the Bible. In these chapters I hope I have been able to give a glimpse of how scholars work, and how the results of scholarship, even in this highly specialized area, can be related to ordinary Christian life and thinking today. The business of building bridges between scholarship and Christian teaching is one which has concerned me for many years. If the present gulf continues the results could be disastrous; we shall have Churches divorced from specialist knowledge of the Christian tradition, and scholars with no concern for the tradition whose texts they study.

It will be clear from these pages that scholarship is international and knows no denominational barriers. The skills required are too many, and the task too great, for everything not to be shared for a common good. The story of the recovery of Enoch illustrates well just how widely the net has to be cast if our heritage is to be recovered and kept.

Chapter 1

The Lost Prophet

The Epistle of Jude (vv. 14–15) mentions Enoch the prophet:

> Enoch in the seventh generation from Adam prophesied, saying, 'Behold the Lord came with his holy myriads, to execute judgment on all, and to convict all the ungodly of all their deeds of ungodliness which they have committed in such an ungodly way, and of all the harsh things which ungodly sinners have spoken against him.'

But there is no book of the prophet Enoch in the Old Testament. Until recently, all that we knew of Enoch was in Genesis 5.18–24. He was the son of Jared and the father of Methuselah; he walked with God and he was not, for God took him. (God is perhaps better translated 'angels', since the word in the Hebrew is the same.) That is all the Old Testament tells us about him, yet books and visions in his name had once been widely known and very influential. It is clear that there was more to the figure than appeared in Genesis, and a considerable cult of Enoch did undoubtedly exist, even though the biblical writers gave no place to it. A belief grew that he did not die; like Elijah he was taken up to heaven. Enoch was to be revealed in the last days as a messenger of judgement. In the Old Testament it was Elijah who was the prophet of the judgement (Mal. 4.5–6), but in later traditions Elijah and Enoch share that role. This role of Enoch is similar to the early Christian belief about Jesus; he was to be kept in heaven until the appointed time for his coming as the Messiah (Acts 3.19–21).

The figure of Enoch attracted a great deal of legendary material over the years, and the nature of this material is most interesting. In Jewish medieval writings he became an almost messianic figure, although in the early Christian centuries Jewish writers had condemned him, perhaps because he was so important for the newly emerging Christians. The medieval Jewish Enoch lived in a secret place, but was summoned by an angel to teach men the ways of God. All who heard his teaching acclaimed him as their king. As his reward, God made him king over the angels. The angels did not take kindly to having a human lord, but Enoch was installed with magnificent robes and a crown. This exaltation bears a strong resemblance to the Christian description of the exaltation of Christ, and the secret of the hidden Enoch is very similar to the early Christian idea (e.g. Mark 1.44; 3.12) that the Messiah had to be kept a secret.

In earlier Jewish tradition Enoch had been less spectacular, but still important. He was a wise man, to whom the angels revealed the secrets of the judgement and the secrets of the natural order. He was especially associated with astronomy and the calendar. He was also a priest who tried to intercede for the fallen angels, and he was the heavenly scribe who presided over the books at the last judgement. Last, but not least, he was given the title Son of Man, another important link to the Christian tradition.

Early Christian tradition also knew Enoch as the great scribe. A fourth-century Coptic work, the Apocalypse of Paul, describes how Paul was taken up into heaven, as in 2 Corinthians 12.2–4. An angel there introduced him to Enoch the scribe of justice. More frequently he is depicted as one of the two prophets who oppose the antichrist in the last days. Revelation 11.3–12 describes these two witnesses, two prophets who oppose the antichrist. They are killed, raised to life again, and then taken to heaven on clouds. The prophets were identified with Enoch and Elijah. Christian writings in many languages – Latin, Greek, Arabic, Coptic, Ethiopic – show how widely this aspect of the Enoch legend was known. Enoch and Elijah also appear together in mystical writings: a woman visionary in twelfth-century France described them as two men with long beards; a woman visionary in fifteenth-century Ethiopia also 'met' Enoch and Elijah. Occasionally, too, Enoch appears in Christian art. An illustration in a twelfth-century Greek manuscript, now in St Catherine's Monastery on Sinai, shows the figure of Death turning away from Enoch. He also appears on a stained glass window in Canterbury Cathedral.

There are several writings associated with Enoch. The names by which they are now known have been given to them by modern scholars in order to distinguish them; they are not their ancient names. The Secrets of Enoch, known as 2 Enoch, is a work which has survived only in Old Church Slavonic, the language of the Russian Church. It could be as old as the New Testament; nobody knows. Hebrew Enoch, known as 3 Enoch, is a Jewish mystical text from perhaps the fourth or fifth century AD. Again, nobody can be certain. The Book of Enoch with which we are concerned here is 1 Enoch, also known as Ethiopic Enoch, because the whole text has survived only in that language. (I say the whole text, but we do not really know the extent of the ancient Enochic writings. It would be more accurate to say 'a large text' of Enoch.) This Enochic literature known in Ethiopic was originally written in Aramaic or possibly Hebrew, and translated at some stage into Greek. Now that we have the Qumran fragments of this work, we know that it was written before the third century BC; it could be much older. It was used by the earliest Christians, then condemned in Western Christendom, and later lost.

For a long time all that was known of 1 Enoch was from quotations by early Christian writers. The Epistle of Barnabas, written about AD 140, quotes from Enoch twice, but without mentioning the source. In Egypt there was a great Christian teacher at the end of the second century, Clement of Alexandria, who was head of the Christian school there. He knew 1 Enoch's account of the fall of the angels, their heavenly knowledge and their earthly wives. Origen, said by the church historian Eusebius to have been a pupil of Clement, also knew Enoch. He knew that 1 Enoch told of incarnate heavenly beings before the time of Christ, but he also tells us that the Book of Enoch was not considered by the Churches to be 'divine'. Irenaeus also knew 1 Enoch. He had come from Smyrna (modern Izmir in Turkey) and became bishop of Lyons in southern France. These men all wrote in Greek. Tertullian wrote in Latin; he was born in Carthage in north Africa, and he considered 1 Enoch to be Scripture. He quoted it in several places in his writings. From these few examples (there are others) it can be seen that 1 Enoch was known and used all over the Christian world in the second century. But then it fell out of favour. Several later writers condemned it. Augustine was bishop of Hippo in north Africa at the beginning of the fifth century. He said that Enoch contained so much falsehood that it had no canonical authority. He admitted that some of it must have been inspired because the apostle Jude said so, but he thought the Hebrew people had been wise to leave it out of their Scriptures. Enoch, he said, was suspiciously old, claiming to have been written by a man only seven generations from Adam! (City of God 15.23). The Apostolic Constitution also condemn Enoch and books like it. They are attributed to Clement, who was bishop of Rome at the end of the first century, but were probably written in Syria at the end of the fourth century. Books like 1 Enoch were deadly and contrary to the truth. Their teaching was to be shunned (Apostolic Constitutions 6.16). One wonders why Enoch aroused such anger, but after condemnation such as that it is hardly surprising that it disappeared from use in the Western Church.

There are also Jewish Christian works which mention Enoch. (By Jewish Christian, I mean Jewish works taken over and adapted by Christians.) The Testaments of the Twelve Patriarchs is one such work. We do not know when it was written, but it is a collection of death-bed speeches attributed to each of Jacob's sons. Testaments such as these were a popular literary form; we have one in the Fourth Gospel, where Jesus speaks at length to his disciples after the Last Supper. The Testament of Dan warns against apostasy and falling under the influence of Satan. He had read predictions of this in the book of Enoch the Righteous. Now that we have the Ethiopic version of 1 Enoch, we can identify many of the quotations in the early Christian and Jewish Christian writings. We can also find what may be allusions to Enochic material in other places, but this is a less certain process than actually identifying a quotation.

In addition, there are ancient texts which quote 'Enoch', but not any Enoch text that we know. The Testament of Simeon says Enoch predicted war between the sons of Simeon and the sons of Levi. The Testament of Levi knew a passage in which Enoch predicted the future corruption of the Levitical priesthood. The Testament of Judah knew a prophecy that Judah would be evil. The Testament of Benjamin and the Testament of Naphtali predicted, on the basis of Enoch, that their descendants would fall into evil ways. We cannot place any of these in known Enochic texts, and we can only assume that there must have been far more Enochic literature than we now know.

Our main source of information has been the Ethiopic version of Enoch which was discovered by James Bruce, a Scottish explorer. He set out on his travels in June 1768, and landed in Ethiopia in September 1769, after many adventures. He describes in his journals how he found the ancient Christian civilization of Ethiopia. It was a land full of churches. Every great man, he says, felt obliged to build one. They were all on hilltops, surrounded by cedar trees, and they were round buildings with thatched roofs. The interiors of the churches were hung with pictures, but carvings were forbidden, as they were deemed a breach of the second commandment. And in their Old Testament, he discovered that they had the long-lost book of Enoch the prophet.

How had it come to Ethiopia? Indeed, how had Christianity come to Ethiopia? Nobody really knows; we have to guess as best we can.

Ethiopia certainly had ancient links with Judaism. The royal house of Ethiopia claims descent from King Solomon. The Queen of Sheba, who visited Solomon, had had a son by him who became the Ethiopian king Menelik. Jewish priests served in his capital city Aksum. The account in Acts 8.26–39 is not the helpful clue it might seem to be, because the eunuch was not an Ethiopian. He was a civil servant of the kingdom of Meroë, to the north of Ethiopia. The two were often confused. The account in Acts is accurate in giving the name of the queen as Candace, but this was the title of the queens of Meroë. There was no woman ruler in Ethiopia. We have therefore to rely on tradition to discover how Ethiopia became Christian.

Some traditions say Matthew preached there; others say it was Bartholomew. The first firm evidence is from the early fourth century, when two young Christian travellers from Tyre stopped at an Ethiopian port to take on supplies. Robbers attacked the ship; only the two young men escaped with their lives. Frumentius and Aedesius were taken captive to Aksum, where they won the people's confidence, and preached Christianity. Eventually they gained the favour of the royal family, and became tutors to the young princes. When the king died, Frumentius was nominated as regent for the young king. Later he returned to Alexandria to recruit more missionaries, and he was then consecrated bishop of Ethiopia. In the later part of his reign King Ezana himself was converted. His earlier royal inscriptions had pagan motifs; the later ones were Christian. A century later there was an influx of Christian refugees after the Council of Chalcedon in 451. The Monophysite Christians found themselves persecuted as heretics. (Monophysite Christians believe that the nature of Jesus is wholly divine, not divine and human.) Many found refuge beyond the reach of the Byzantine emperors, and among the refugees were nine monks with Syrian names who were so successful as missionaries in Ethiopia that they were made saints. They founded monasteries and translated sacred books. Perhaps this is how Enoch came to Ethiopia.

As Bruce travelled in Ethiopia he collected such manuscripts as he could purchase, and commissioned scribes to copy out others for him. He was recommended a certain scribe of the Law who would be able to copy the holy books for him. In his journal (*Travels to Discover the Source of the Nile*, vol. vii, 2nd ed., Edinburgh 1804) we find the entry:

December 12 1770. Weleda Yesous the younger has undertaken to

write the books of Joshua and Judges and has received three quires
of four leaves each and two salts on account of his pay.

It appears that Bruce provided the parchment for the scribes daily as
they worked. Other scribes copied other works. At the end of his
journey he reported:

> Amongst the articles I consigned to the library at Paris, was a very
> beautiful and magnificent copy of the prophecies of Enoch, in large
> quarto; another is amongst the books of scripture which I brought
> home, standing immediately before the book of Job, which is its
> proper place in the Abyssinian canon; and a third copy I have
> presented to the Bodleian Library in Oxford by the hands of Dr
> Douglas, the Bishop of Carlisle. (*Travels*, vol ii)

He gives a brief résumé of the book for his readers, and describes how
the angels fell in love with the daughters of men and had children by
them. The children were fearful giants who destroyed the earth:
'These giants were not so charitable to the sons and daughters of men
as their fathers had been.'

The first translation of 1 Enoch into English was made by Laurence
in 1821, using the manuscripts brought back by Bruce. During the
early nineteenth century many more manuscripts of Enoch had been
brought to Europe, but the next real development did not come until
1886, when a Greek manuscript of 1 Enoch 1–32 was discovered by
archaeologists in Egypt. Until this discovery, the only evidence for
1 Enoch in Greek had been very fragmentary. There were the quotations in the early Christian writers; there was a short extract from
Enoch 89 discovered in an eleventh-century manuscript in the Vatican; and there was the writing of a Byzantine Greek historian, George
Syncellus. (Syncellus is a title not a name; it means someone who
shares a cell with another monk, a companion.) Little is known of him
apart from the fact that he was the secretary to Tarasius, Patriarch of
Constantinople 784–806. He had spent some of his life in Palestine,
and after service with the patriarch he retired to a monastery to write a
history of the world. He used parts of Enoch in his description of the
time before Noah's flood, and he quotes from chapters 6–10 and
15–16, which tell the tale of the fallen angels and their judgement. It is
generally thought that his monastery library did not contain a complete text of Enoch, but that he quoted extracts from an earlier work
by a fifth-century Alexandrian monk, Panodorus. These quotations

from the Greek Enoch were first noticed by J. Scaliger, who published his work in Amsterdam in 1658. Thus at the end of the seventeenth century we had in Greek only chapters 6–11, 15–16, 89, and several quotations.

In the winter of 1886–7, a Coptic Christian cemetery was excavated at Akhmim, a town situated in upper Egypt on the banks of the Nile, about two hundred and fifty miles south of Cairo. The cemetery was in a hillside over two miles long, and it was honeycombed with rock graves. Buried with the dead were grave goods. Beautiful tapestries were found, some of them dating from the second and third centuries AD, making them the earliest known examples of this type of work. In one grave a small book was found containing the Gospel of Peter, the Apocalypse of Peter and almost all the first part of Enoch (chs 1–32) bound together in one volume. It was only a small book, thirty-three pages of parchment measuring 16cm. × 13cm., but it was the longest text of Enoch known in Greek, and dates from the fifth or sixth century. Then in 1930 fourteen pages of a fourth-century papyrus codex of Enoch were discovered and acquired. They represent the last section of Enoch, known as the Epistle of Enoch, and they are now in Dublin. Thus we have now managed to piece together quite a large amount of the Greek text of Enoch.

Work soon began on a new translation. The scholar who undertook the work was Robert Henry Charles, an Irishman born in County Tyrone in 1855. He was to become the giant figure in Enoch scholarship, and his work has yet to be surpassed. He was educated in Belfast and Dublin, and was then ordained and worked in London parishes for six years. Due to ill health he went to Germany for a year, where his interest in intertestamental literature began. When he returned to England he settled in Oxford, and in 1893 published the first edition of his translation of Enoch. The second edition, which appeared in 1912, became the standard text, and until recently was the only one in use in English. (His version of 1 Enoch is the one quoted in this book.) He said that Enoch was 'The most important Jewish work written between 200 BC and AD 100.' Other works of scholarship followed; Charles made many apocalyptic texts available to scholars for the first time, and in so doing altered for ever the face of biblical scholarship. In order to do this he had to be a master not only of Hebrew, Greek and Latin, but also of Syriac, Armenian and Ethiopic. His obituary said that nothing he wrote on the subject of apocalyptic literature could safely be ignored, and this is still true. He was

honoured with many awards and distinctions: in 1925 he was the first
to receive the British Academy's medal for biblical studies. In 1913 he
was made a canon of Westminster, and in 1919 became Archdeacon.
Ten years later he was seriously injured in a road accident, and after
eighteen months of disability he died on 30 January 1931.

The most exciting and significant development in Enochic study
came in September 1952. Five years previously, the first of the Dead
Sea Scrolls had been found in caves near ruins of the Qumran
monastery, at the north-western corner of the Dead Sea. (The place is
sometimes called Hirbet Qumran; *hirbet* means 'ruin of'.) The story of
the discovery is well known; an Arab shepherd-boy looking for a lost
goat amused himself by throwing stones up into the mouths of the
caves. From one he heard the sound of breaking pottery. After
recovering from his fear, he and a friend investigated, crawled in
through the narrow mouth of the cave, and found a row of eight
earthenware jars, one of which contained three scrolls. One of these
was later found to be a complete scroll of the prophet Isaiah. When it
was discovered that these could be sold for good money, further secret
visits were made, and soon there was a steady supply of fragments
offered for sale to learned institutions. The Syrian Metropolitan in St
Mark's Monastery, Mar Athanasius, bought some of them and took
them to the United States, but it proved difficult to find a buyer, and
they were eventually purchased by the State of Israel in 1955 for a
quarter of a million dollars. A professor at the Hebrew University,
E. L. Sukenik, had recognized the age of the scrolls, and their
importance, but there was a war going on between Jews and Arabs and
life was not easy. When a truce was agreed in July 1948 archaeologists
were able to make a thorough search of the cave, and it was properly
cleaned. One of the works found then was a rewriting of Genesis,
named by scholars the Genesis Apocryphon. (We shall see the significance of this text in chapter 3.)

One evening in 1952 a group of Arab herdsmen were discussing the
finds, and their new-found source of income, when a very old man
among them remembered an incident in his youth. He had been
hunting in that area and had followed a wounded partridge into a cave.
He had found his prey, and also an old lamp and several fragments of
pottery. The listening men noted all the details that the old man could
remember as to the location of the cave. Then they set out. They
found the cave, dug in the earth of the floor, and came to a thick layer
of thousands of manuscript fragments. Unfortunately for them, but

THE LOST PROPHET

fortunately for scholars, rival tribesmen revealed the whereabouts of the cave, and a team of experts was able to sift out and recover many valuable fragments. The cave of the partridge, known as Cave 4, seems to have been the library of the Qumran settlement, or the place where they stored their library when the disaster struck which forced them to abandon their settlement and hide their scrolls. It was an artificial cave, and had at one time been a hermit's cell. One of the two chambers had been stacked almost full of jars containing manuscripts. Some of these had been torn, but the tears were very old, suggesting that the cave had been robbed many centuries previously. Among the fragments were the remains of eleven manuscripts, or part manuscripts, of 1 Enoch. (A complete account of the early discoveries can be read in J. T. Milik, *Ten Years of Discovery in the Wilderness of Judaea*, London 1959.)

Not all of the Ethiopic text was represented. The Book of Enoch is usually divided into five sections (see Chapter 2), and all sections but one were represented among the pieces. The second section of the Ethiopic text, known as the Similitudes of Enoch, was not there. This is a very significant gap, as we shall see later, because the Similitudes are a very close relation to much in early Christian thought, and the question which all scholars would like to answer is: 'Were they a Christian composition, or were they an older work which the Christians used?' It is possible that they were not written until after the Qumran library had been abandoned. It is also possible that the library did not have a copy of every known Enochic work. Another distinct possibility is that the caves had been visited in the past, and books removed. Origen, the great Christian scholar and teacher who lived in Caesarea in the early third century and who died a martyr's death in the persecution of AD 254, found a translation of the Book of Psalms together with other Hebrew and Greek books in a jar near Jericho. Jericho is about ten miles north of Qumran! At the end of the eighth century the Patriarch of Seleucia knew of Old Testament books and others in Hebrew writing which had been found in a rock-dwelling near Jericho by an Arab out hunting who followed his dog into a cave. (Seleucia was the port of Antioch; Paul and his companions embarked there on their missionary journey, Acts 13.4.) A ninth-century writer knew of a Jewish sect called 'the Sect of the Cave' because their books were found in a cave. The twentieth-century scholars, then, were not the first to take scrolls from the ancient library of Qumran, and it would be very dangerous to assume that what was not there in the 1950s had never been there in the first place.

The fragments of Enoch which were found really were fragments. Some of the usable pieces were half the size of a normal postage stamp! These had to be sorted and identified before the task of translation could begin. The work involved was enormous, and a full edition of the fragments was not ready for publication until 1976, twenty-four years after they had been found (J. T. Milik, *The Books of Enoch. Aramaic Fragments of Qumran Cave 4*, Oxford 1976). The pieces had to be distinguished from each other in various ways. Not all the parchments were the same colour. Some were cream, others light brown, some had a bluish tinge, others were slightly pink, depending on the colour of the skin which had made the parchment. In addition, there were several different handwritings; in many cases individual scribes could be identified, and their work collected on that basis. Ink colours differed, as did the style of the lettering, and even the way in which the guide-lines for the writing had been drawn. Eventually the legible pieces were translated, and the partly legible ones were reconstructed. The gaps were filled in order to give a sensible reading, although when a filled gap is printed in a translation it is always printed within square brackets so that the reader knows what it is. More often than not there is more gap than text, but the reconstruction is based upon the size of the letters and the length of each column line in the scroll. The translator then knows how many letters have to fit between the groups of letters which he does have, representing perhaps a column which has been torn in half down its middle, or even partially eaten away. It is a very skilled business.

Once the fragments had been assembled and translated, the task of comparing Aramaic and Ethiopic began. The correspondence was remarkably good, showing that the Ethiopic version is substantially the same as the version which was used by the Qumran community, even though in some parts the Aramaic is fuller than the Ethiopic. For example, the third section, the Astronomy Book, is longer in the Aramaic than in the Ethiopic, and suggests that the Enochic literature had once been far greater than its present remains. Of course there are differences between the versions, but these are the concern of professional scholars of Aramaic, Greek and Ethiopic. The general sense of the text is immediately clear from any of the English versions.

Since the Aramaic fragments were discovered there has been a great increase in scholarly activity. The study of the pseudepigrapha (1 Enoch and similar works) is the fastest-growing area of biblical scholarship, and a knowledge of 1 Enoch is now a necessary preliminary to any responsible study of the New Testament.

There are three translations of Enoch readily available in English:

R. H. Charles, *The Book of Enoch* (Oxford 1912; SPCK 1917, repr. 1987), also incorporated in his *Apocrypha and Pseudepigrapha of the Old Testament*, vol. ii; Pseudepigrapha (Oxford 1913).

M. A. Knibb, *The Ethiopic Book of Enoch* (Oxford 1978), also incorporated in H. D. F. Sparks (ed.), *The Apocryphal Old Testament* (Oxford 1984). The latter is a revision of Charles's Pseudepigrapha.

E. Isaac in J. H. Charlesworth (ed.), *The Old Testament Pseudepigrapha. vol. i: Apocalyptic Literature and Testaments* (New York and London 1983).

Chapter 2

The Book of Enoch

The Book of Enoch is very strange. It describes heavenly visions, journeys through fantastic mountain ranges to see the fiery pit where evil angels burn, the last judgement before the great throne, and the movements of the sun and stars. Some parts are very like the prophets in the Old Testament; others tell curiously unfamiliar versions of the history of Israel. How do we begin to cope with such a book, and why should we even try?

The shock of its strangeness can be a very good thing. We know that the Book of Enoch is strange, that it needs explanation, that it belongs to another age and another way of thinking and speaking about God. We also know that this same book was used and understood by the people who wrote the New Testament: Enoch the prophet is quoted at Jude 14, and the theme of Enoch is taken up in 2 Peter 2. There are many places, as we shall see later, where Enoch lies very close to the surface of the New Testament, but these two very clear and obvious examples will do for now. If the New Testament writers were quite at home in the world of Enoch, which seems to us so utterly strange and incomprehensible, how can we be sure that we are reading and understanding the New Testament in the way that was originally intended? Might there be more to the familiar texts than first meets the eye? Might the very familiarity of the New Testament texts mean that we read them in our way, and not in their way? Unguided Bible study can be a very mixed blessing, and easily lead to creating God in our own image. It is one thing to read the New Testament in modern, everyday English, but quite another to understand it, because it was not written with modern, everyday English ideas.

Reading Enoch in modern English illustrates this problem perfectly, and brings us face to face with a whole body of literature for which we have not devised our own ways of understanding, and our own selection of what we can and cannot cope with. There is no doubt that there are, for example, some passages in the New Testament which are nowadays used more frequently than others. They seem more relevant, more important. We make a selection from Scripture, and therefore, inevitably, a distortion. You will hear more sermons from Romans 5 than you will from Jude, more from Luke 10.29–36, the good Samaritan, than from the preceding section which tells of the judgement on Capernaum, Satan falling from heaven, and treading on scorpions. This is because Jude and the last judgement are no longer comfortable for us. But does this selection process really distort the New Testament? Surely it must. With 1 Enoch we may be tempted to do the same thing, and pick out familiar-sounding sections which deal with social justice and the like because we can cope with them. If we do do this, we shall be missing a great opportunity to alter our mental picture of the whole thought-world of Jesus' time.

We have given ourselves the familiar picture of Jesus the simple teacher surrounded by ordinary and largely unlettered folk who withstood the sophisticated religious leaders of their time. The setting is a Galilee of boats and sheep, even though Galilee in those times was a place of resistance fighters and bloody ambushes, and hopes for the final end of Roman rule. The points at which Enoch illuminates the New Testament show that ours is far from being an accurate picture. 1 Enoch is not a popular work, not the simple religion of Galilean peasants and fishermen. It represents an enormous body of learning, sophisticated in its own way – ancient, intricate and highly developed. If teachings such as these were known to the New Testament writers, then the New Testament itself may be no more than the tip of an iceberg. A great deal of what was important in early Christianity may not be spelt out in the New Testament because it was already accepted. We may be basing our picture of the teachings of the first Christians on a very small part of what they actually were. Much of the theology developed by the early Churches may have been no more than unpacking what was already there from the start. Thus we owe it to ourselves to make some sort of effort to understand this curious book, and the others like it.

The Enoch after whom the book is named was a wise man from the age before Noah's flood. The words of this book are attributed to him even though he cannot possibly have written it. Such a practice is known as pseudepigraphy, 'writing under a false name'. To the modern mind it seems like forgery, but if we allow this to colour our judgements, many other things will come as an even greater shock. Writing in the name of another, claiming prophetic inspiration in this way, was an accepted thing in New Testament times. One of the most dramatic of the Dead Sea Scrolls, and the largest, is the Temple

Scroll, and this is written as a new divine revelation to Moses. Deuteronomy was probably composed in the same way, although much earlier, since both are revisions of the Law given to Moses. We do not think of biblical writings as pseudepigraphical, but many of them are. An early Christian hymnbook is called the Odes of Solomon; Solomon did not write them. Similarly the Book of Revelation shows us the seer John being instructed in his vision to write down the words of the heavenly Jesus, and send them to the seven churches as a message from Jesus (Rev. 1.11; 2.1,8, etc.). It is quite possible that much of the Fourth Gospel is also words from the heavenly Jesus given to an early Christian prophet, as the infant Churches began to realize the true significance of Jesus. The incident on the road to Emmaus shows us that the disciples had not understood about Jesus during his earthly ministry; all the interpretation of his work was done with the wisdom of hindsight. Perhaps the best example of all is Paul, who was adamant that the gospel he had received came direct from Jesus, even though he had not known Jesus at all during his earthly ministry (Gal. 1.11–12). This custom of prophetic pseudepigraphy is not one that should bother us unduly; it is just one more example of how the ways of those times differed from ours. Eventually the practice was curbed by emphasis on the apostolic tradition, the direct line of teaching derived from apostles who had been eyewitnesses of Jesus' ministry, but the tension continued in the conflict between those who said that everything had to be provable from Scripture, and those who said that there were other sources for Christian teaching and belief.

The Book of Enoch has many points of contact with the Old Testament, but even more points where it is very different. It has no place for the elaborate sacrificial cult of the temple, no actual quotation from the Old Testament as we know it (except for the song of the angels, 'Holy, Holy Holy' which is the same as in Isa. 6.3), and it has no great role for the Law of Moses. What type of Judaism was this which had no real place for the Law and none for the sacrificial cult? What it does have is a great emphasis on the day of judgement, and the mediation and revelation of Enoch, who was a wise man, a scribe and a priest. It has many points of contact with Isaiah and the Psalms, and seems to have kept alive many ancient traditions which have faded from prominence in the Old Testament books. 1 Enoch itself says that the changes and developments after the Jewish people came back from Babylon were a bad thing. Those who built the new temple were impure and apostate:

And they began again to build as before, and they reared up that tower, and it was named the high tower; and they began again to place a table before the tower, but all the bread on it was polluted and not pure . . .

And after that in the seventh week shall an apostate generation arise,
And many shall be its deeds,
And all its deeds shall be apostate. (1 Enoch 89.73; 93.9)

This implies that what we have in Enoch is the writing of a very conservative group whose roots go right back to the time of the first temple, when there were still kings in Jerusalem. If this is correct, it is of very great importance for our understanding of Christianity, for the central theme of Christianity is that Jesus was the Messiah, the Anointed, the true king of Israel. Early Christianity always claimed to be the true fulfilment of the Old Testament; what could have been more natural than for the ideas about the Messiah to have been based upon the ancient hopes and ideals of the earlier kings? In Enoch we almost certainly have an echo of these earlier ways, and Enoch has been preserved only as a Christian book, even though it was written long before the time of Jesus. The Christian Churches saw some special importance in this work, and it influenced much of their thinking about the Messiah.

The later fate of Enoch confirms this. Some Jewish teachers in the earliest Christian centuries had a very negative attitude towards it. A commentary on Genesis (Genesis Rabbah 25.1) says Enoch was wicked and hypocritical, that he was taken up by God before he had the chance to fall into more bad ways. Other traditions, however, remember him as the great scribe in heaven (e.g. the Jerusalem Talmud to Genesis 5.2). He became the archangel Metatron (3 Enoch 4–16). He was a messianic figure, the agent of God (3 Enoch 10.3–6). Enoch was a figure who aroused considerable passions. Scholars in general agree that the Old Testament reference to Enoch at Genesis 5.21–24 is cryptic, and implies that the writer knew more about him than he chose to include. The Genesis account of the fallen angels (Gen. 6.1–4) has also been heavily edited; the Hebrew does not run smoothly. Even as early as the writing of Genesis, it looks as though there was hostility to Enoch and the tradition associated with him. Despite this there were those who cherished the traditions, and among them were the Christians. Does this mean that those who were the first Christian converts had an existing quarrel with certain sectors of Judaism? Perhaps 1 Enoch gives us a clue as to the nature of the quarrel? Was Jesus not the cause of the division, but rather the agent of its finalization? This type of exploration of Enoch has been compared to the work of an archaeologist who uses aerial photographs, and from markings still visible on the surface is able to discover where to dig in order to recover what would otherwise have remained hidden.

When we compare Enoch with other ancient writings not in the Old Testament, we discover that many of them have allusions to the same old traditions as we find in Enoch. If they were all identical, we could perhaps say that one writing had copied from another, but since the relationship between them is very complicated, we can only conclude that we have in them pieces of an ancient jigsaw of ideas, which, when put together, give a picture of what underlies much of the Old Testament. Nowhere is this clearly spelt out in the biblical books, but this may only mean that it was common knowledge, too well known to need comment. This hidden pattern underlies the New Testament also.

We find this pattern in several books written in the second century BC, for example in the Book of Jubilees, a rewriting of Genesis; in the Assumption of Moses, a rewriting of the last part of Deuteronomy; in the Testament of Judah, which purports to be the last words of Jacob's son Judah before his death; and in a few allusions in the biblical Daniel. The picture they give is very important for our understanding of the world-view of the New Testament writers. They describe the last judgement as a great trial before the throne of God, and the struggle between two angel princes, one good and one evil. Jude 9 tells of Michael and Satan disputing over the possession of Moses' body; this is the same pattern of ideas. Or we might be reminded of the Fourth Gospel's picture of the Holy Spirit as the Advocate in the great trial. The lost tradition also tells how a great book is opened, and the wicked receive their just reward. The righteous, often called the wise, receive eternal life, which is described as exaltation to the stars or as an ascension to look down on the judgement of their enemies. The wicked are cast down to their punishment in a fiery pit. The Book of Revelation is clearly in this tradition, as are Jesus' words, 'I saw Satan fall like lightning from heaven' (Luke 10.18). Jesus was one who had ascended to the presence of God; he had been there when the evil angel was thrown down.

Many people who say the creeds, with their references to the last judgement and life everlasting, give very little thought to what is actually meant by those words. We have come to some arrangement with ourselves as to what those words mean, or can reasonably be expected to mean in the twentieth century, in order to save ourselves from the literalism of the fundamentalists, and those curious minorities who try to calculate the date of the last judgement or the actual identity of the various dragons. But when we look at these ideas of judgement in their original settings, we find that they are remarkably sophisticated, and, when properly unpacked, very relevant to the twentieth century.

The Book of Enoch is divided into five sections, known as the Book of the Watchers, the Similitudes, the Astronomy Book, the Book of Dreams, and the Epistle of Enoch. All but the second section have been found as fragments among the Dead Sea Scrolls, and the fact that the Similitudes have not been found there has created a heated argument among scholars. The Similitudes, also known as the Parables, contain much material which seems to be very Christian. There are, for example, passages about someone called the Son of Man, and his role in the last judgement. If the Similitudes are a Christian work, then these Son of Man passages describe early Christian belief as it developed from the gospel references to Jesus as Son of Man. But if the Similitudes are a pre-Christian work, then we have in them a picture of what the earliest Christians might have understood about Jesus when they used the title Son of Man to describe him, or what Jesus might have meant when he called himself Son of Man. (We shall explore this further in chapter 7.) Those who say that the Similitudes are post-Christian point to the Dead Sea Scrolls as strong evidence. The Similitudes are not there, therefore they must have been composed later. But this is a dangerous argument, unless we can be certain that the Qumran library had a copy of every known book, which is unlikely. There are other 'Enoch' writings quoted in the Testaments of the Twelve Patriarchs (a second-century BC work), and in the early Christian Epistle of Barnabas, but we cannot match these quotations to any known Enoch book, let alone to those among the Dead Sea Scrolls. This means that the Qumran library had some Enoch books, but not all of them. The Similitudes may have been among those it did not have.

The question of dating the other Enoch books is also vexed. A common method has been to analyse the fragments found at Qumran, and thus to date the books, but this is a dangerous practice. If we could prove that the Enoch books were actually composed at Qumran, and that these surviving bits were from the author's actual manuscript, then the physical remains could date the texts to the second or third century BC. But we can do no such thing. Imagine what this method of dating would do for the Old Testament. Our earliest physical proofs for the existence of the Old Testament, pieces of ancient scroll we can see and handle, are also among the Dead Sea Scrolls. Does this mean that the Old Testament books were all composed in the second century BC in the Qumran monastery? It is unlikely! We must not have one set of rules for the biblical texts and another for the non-biblical. The Enoch writings could be as old as anything in the Old Testament. We must keep an open mind.

The first section, *The Book of the Watchers*, takes its name from the Watchers, the angels who came to earth and corrupted it. In the customary chapter numberings this section is chapters 1–34, but not all the material is one consistent piece. It is a compilation, rather as the stories in Genesis and Exodus are a compilation; and even within the smaller units there are signs that older materials have been joined together. Inconsistencies have been left, just as they have been in Genesis. If you read the Genesis account of Noah's flood, it is obvious that you are reading two versions of the same story at the same time. (Does Noah take two of each type of animal, Gen. 6.19; 7.9, or does he take seven pairs, Gen. 7.2? Does the flood last forty days, Gen. 7.17, or does it last one hundred and fifty days, Gen. 7.24?) This type of inconsistency does not seem to have worried the ancient authors. We find exactly the same thing in Enoch. The earliest part of the Book of Watchers, chapters 6–10, tells two interwoven stories about the fall of the evil angels. One describes how Asael brought heavenly knowledge to earth, and with it corrupted the creation. He taught about metallurgy and cosmetics – 'eternal secrets' (these perhaps seem rather an odd choice of eternal secrets!) – and was eventually bound by the archangel Raphael. He was imprisoned in the desert under a heap of jagged rocks until the time of the great judgement, when he was destined for the fire. We should like to know more about this Asael; he appears in other places in Enoch. In the Similitudes he appears at 55.4, where he is judged by the Elect One as the leader of the evil angels, and yet in 69.2 he is only the twenty-first leader of the bands of angel rebels. In the Book of Dreams he appears as a fallen star, the first to fall from heaven. The story there suggests that it was Asael who corrupted Adam and Eve in the Garden of Eden, by encouraging them to want knowledge which had been forbidden to them. The story as we have it now in Genesis 2–3 certainly seems to have a great deal missing from it. We are never told, for example, how the newly created garden came to have an evil serpent in it. Enoch tells us how he got there and who he really was.

There is a desert demon in Leviticus 16.6–10 with a similar name – Azazel. The ancient ritual of the scapegoat required that a goat be sent into the wilderness to Azazel. The goat carried all the transgressions and sins of Israel into the wilderness, to Azazel (Lev. 16.20–22). The Old Testament tells us nothing more about Azazel, or why he was in the wilderness. He must have been important, as he is the only one apart from God to whom a sacrifice is to be offered, and it was thought appropriate to send sins to him, out in the desert. In Enoch we find that Asael, the fallen leader of the angels, is imprisoned in the wilderness. Enoch tells us how he got there, and who he really was.

The other story of the fallen angels in chapters 6–10 tells how two hundred of them led by Semihazah bound themselves by a great oath, and then descended to the earth to marry human wives. Their offspring were fearful demons, who infested and corrupted the earth. Their fate was to be bound by the archangel Michael for seventy generations in the valleys of the earth, to see their demon children destroy each other, and then be led off to the abyss of fire at the last judgement. It is the demon offspring of Semihazah's angels whom we meet in the Gospels, still infesting the earth, and fearing when they are driven out by Jesus, that the judgement has come too early (Matt. 8.29). After the judgement on the Watchers, the creation is released from their power, and restored to fertility and prosperity.

These two stories are told in the Book of the Watchers without any mention of Enoch. They are simply the setting for what happens next. Then, in chapter 12, we learn that Enoch is to take to the fallen ones the message of their judgement. Enoch, like the other prophets, is commissioned to announce the imminent judgement of God. Unlike the other prophets, he announces judgement upon the evil angels. The fallen ones ask Enoch to intercede for them, and Enoch is then caught up to heaven in a vision of God. What follows is one of the most remarkable passages in the book (we shall return to it later). In his heavenly vision Enoch learns that there is to be no mercy for the fallen ones.

The remainder of the Book of Watchers describes Enoch's heavenly journeys, when he travels to explore the secrets of the creation. He sees where the stars and the thunders are kept, the sources of the great rivers and the cornerstones of the earth. He sees the place where the evil stars are imprisoned, he sees the heavenly mountains and he sees the Tree of Life. The closest parallel to these journeys is in the biblical book of Job, chapters 38–9. When Job is claiming great wisdom, the Lord speaks to him from a whirlwind and asks if he can know all these secrets of creation. Job admits that he cannot, that such knowledge and the power that it brings belong to God alone. Yet here in Enoch we find that belief contradicted. Enoch is given that heavenly knowledge; and the tradition in which he stands, as we shall see, believed that such knowledge conferred angelic status and made one, in effect, like God. Compare this with Genesis 2–3. In the story of the Garden of Eden the serpent promises Adam and Eve that they would have knowledge to open their eyes and make them like God. Whoever wrote the Genesis story believed that this knowledge was wrong, and the cause of all subsequent evil. Yet the other, lost tradition says that this knowledge brought one to the presence of God. The wise, like Enoch, walked with God.

The second section of Enoch, chapters 37–71, known as *The Similitudes* or *The Parables*, is described as a vision of wisdom. It consists of three separate visions of the great judgement on the kings and the mighty, and is clearly compiled from at least two versions of an older tradition. A figure called the Son of Man, or the Elect One, presides at the great judgement, and at the end of the section we discover that Enoch is to be the Son of Man, the agent of judgement. (Or at least, this is what the text seems to say. If we are dealing with familiar texts and materials, there is sufficient certainty to make an informed choice one way or the other when there is a problem. Here, we just have to admit that there is a very strange reading and we have insufficient knowledge to do anything about it.) There are so many important issues raised by the Similitudes that we shall deal with them later in detail (see chapter 5), and not attempt anything more at this point.

The third section, chapters 72–82, is known as *The Astronomy Book*. The fragments of this section found at Qumran show that it was once far longer than the version we now have. The angel Uriel reveals to Enoch all the laws which govern the movements of the heavenly bodies. It comes as a surprise to us to find that such knowledge is part of a religious treatise, but this is because we separate science and religion and treat them as very different disciplines. In the ancient world this was not so. The wise men – and remember that Enoch was a wise man, a scribe and a priest – were learned in all the knowledge of their day. They knew about medicine and mathematics, metallurgy and engineering, as well as those aspects of knowledge which we should consider more dubious: magic, astrology and reading omens. For them, all knowledge was knowledge of God's creation, and it was important to know and observe these laws of God. Thus in this part of the book Enoch is told about the true calculation of the calendar, which had to be based on the sun. We know that the period of the second temple was a time of many disputes about the calendar; those in the restored community in Jerusalem seem to have adopted a lunar calendar which offended the conservative elements of the population. Under that newer system the days of the sacred festivals fell at a different time, and it was greatly feared that a sacred ritual performed at the wrong time was not effective. The calculations to establish the calendar were complex, and apparently a secret. According to the tradition of the Samaritans, for example, the calendar was regulated by their High Priest, who had all the secret formulae carved on the high priestly staff. We learn nothing about calendar calculations in the Old Testament. Given the importance of the calendar in cultic matters, this is a conspicuous silence.

The most famous of these disputes concerned the introduction of a moon-based calendar, and some of the additional parts of the Astronomy Book found at Qumran do in fact deal with the relationship between solar and lunar calendars. The account as we have it in the Ethiopic version has no polemic about this new calendar; perhaps it comes from a time before this dispute arose, or after it had been resolved. Enoch's Astronomy Book simply warns against leaving out the extra day every quarter which was necessary to keep the calendar even approximately correct. Each season of the year had a patron angel who had his special day, and within each season there were three other angels, each ruling a month of thirty days. Thus each quarter was $3 \times 30 + 1$, i.e. 91 days, giving a year of 364 days. This was exactly fifty-two weeks, to fit with the seven-day week pattern of the Jewish calendar. Sinners, warns the angel, will alter the calendar, so that things will no longer happen at the proper time, the stars will not rise and set when they should, and the whole order of creation will be upset. This is seen as a revolt of the stars against their proper order, i.e. as another manifestation of angelic revolt:

And in the days of the sinners the years shall be shortened,
And their seed shall be tardy on their lands and fields,
And all things on the earth shall alter,

And shall not appear in their time:
And the rain shall be kept back
And the heaven shall withhold it . . .

And the moon shall alter her order,
And not appear at her time . . .

And many chiefs of the stars shall transgress the order (prescribed).
And these shall alter their orbits and tasks,
And not appear at the seasons prescribed to them.

(1 Enoch 80.2, 4, 6)

Nobody can say for certain where this system of reckoning originated. It bears little resemblance to any other known from the ancient world, and may well be peculiar to Israel. The horizon was divided up into a series of 'gates' through which the sun rose, and thus they were able to calculate the time of the year from the position of the rising and setting of the sun. As early as the fourth century BC pagan writers mention the Jews as astronomers, but this aspect of their lives could never have been guessed from the Old Testament.

Another reason for studying the stars was to predict future events. This cannot have been astrology in the modern sense, since all the stars except the evil rebels were bound by the fixed laws of God, as part of the great cosmic covenant (see chapter 6). But the writers of these apocalypses had a curious belief about stars which may give us a clue as to why the wise men were so much in demand as political advisers. The stars represented kings, and each king had his own guardian angel who was also a star. We find hints of this angel/star/king belief even in the Old Testament; it was very ancient, and not something newly borrowed from paganism. Isaiah 14, for example, describes how a proud star, the king of Babylon, is thrown from heaven as punishment for his pride. Ezekiel 28 describes an angel, the king of Tyre, who is also thrown down as punishment for abusing his wisdom. The wise men knew of the fates of kings and they could predict their future in the stars. We can now see why the wise men in

Matthew 2 spoke as they did. They were looking for a new king because they had seen his new star. It is very likely that they were Jewish wise men!

The fourth section of Enoch, chapters 83–90, *The Book of Dreams*, describes two dream-visions which Enoch recounts to his son Methuselah. The first dream is one of the destruction of the earth. The second, told at much greater length, describes the history of Israel. The events are described in increasing detail as the dream approaches the time of the Maccabean revolt in 167 BC, suggesting that the terrifying events of that period were all part of God's plan, the woes to bring about the kingdom of the Messiah and the great judgement. The Book of Daniel also comes from this period, and it, too, has a complex account of Israel's history culminating in the events of the Maccabean revolt. But Daniel and Enoch differ in one important detail: Daniel's history does not end with great judgement, whereas Enoch's does. This is a very clear example of how the Old Testament and the 'lost' tradition differ. Enoch's history, like Daniel's, is told as an animal fable. Adam is a white bull, the twelve sons of Jacob are sheep, the enemies of Israel are eagles, vultures, ravens, and so on. The angel figures in the history are described as 'men' or 'men in white', and there are three notable people who are born as animals and yet become 'men'. Decoded, this means that Noah, Moses and Elijah began life as mortals and achieved the status of angels. This code of 'animals' for human beings and 'men' for angels is important for understanding some parts of the New Testament and early Christian writings. In the Easter stories, for example, Mark describes a man in white at the tomb, and Matthew an angel. Luke has two men in dazzling clothes, John has two angels in white. There is still the problem over the number of figures, but the men in white, or the men in dazzling clothes, were angel figures. The Essenes saw themselves as living the angelic life, and they, too, wore white.

Once we realize that a man in white is an angel figure, one who belongs to heaven and not to earth, several other references and early Christian customs begin to fall into place. We find that acquiring angel status, i.e. eternal life, is symbolized by putting on white garments, and sometimes by anointing with oil, thus linking the angels to the royal figure. The righteous, says Enoch, will wear garments of glory, garments of life (1 Enoch 62.16). Luke 9.29 describes the dazzling white clothes of Jesus at the Transfiguration.

Revelation 3.4–5 mentions those who have not soiled their garments, those who will conquer and walk in heaven in white garments. Revelation 4.4 describes the elders before the throne, clad in white and wearing crowns. There are also white garments mentioned at Revelation 6.11; 7.9,13–14. Sometimes the robing is no more than a figure of speech, as at 1 Corinthians 15.53, where Paul talks of putting on immortality. Elsewhere the imagery is more explicit: 'These are they who have put off mortal clothing and have put on the immortal, and they have confessed the name of God; now they are being crowned and receive palms' (2 Esd. 2.45). Angels often wear crowns; they are royal figures.

Sometimes the robing is developed into an elaborate description of admission into the heavenly state, as in the Ascension of Isaiah, a Jewish Christian work from the end of the first century. Isaiah ascends and passes through each of the seven heavens. He is told that he will receive a robe which will make him the equal of the angels in the highest heaven (Asc. Isa. 8.14; 9.3). He sees Enoch stripped of the robe of flesh, and wearing heavenly robes like angels (Asc. Isa. 9.9); the righteous brought up by the Lord Christ will receive in heaven a robe, a throne and a crown (Asc. Isa. 9.18). 2 Enoch describes how Enoch is given garments of glory by the archangel Michael, and anointed with sweet ointment. This transforms him into an angel (2 Enoch 22.8–10). The second-century African martyr St Satyrus had a vision of heaven. Those who entered the great walls of light were given white robes by the angels as they entered. From earliest times a white robe has been put on after baptism, as a sign of the new life. This garment was often described as the shining garment, denoting the next world, which is shining and radiant, into which the newly baptized had passed. They were called the newly illuminated ones, those who had seen the light, and, like Enoch's angels, were described as stars. Enoch's angelic code 'the men in white' is the key to a great deal of the symbolism and practice of the early Church, and explains our custom of white christening-robes for babies. We also find it in well-known hymns, where their very familiarity often prevents our noticing the words. Isaac Watts's hymn for All Saints' Day has very ancient roots:

> How bright these glorious spirits shine!
> Whence all their bright array?
> How came they to the blissful seats
> Of everlasting day?

As does Alford's:

> Ten thousand times ten thousand,
> In sparkling raiment bright,
> The armies of the ransomed Saints
> Throng up the steeps of light . . .

If we lose touch with our symbolism we are in danger of cutting ourselves off from our roots. It will be like a collective loss of memory, and we shall not know who we are, or why we are here. These ancient pictures all convey a very deep theological insight, from the days when theology was communicated by images and symbols. I was saddened to read recently an account of how traditional Christmas carols are being modernized (*Daily Mail*, 12 November 1987). The clergyman who is modernizing the original versions described the last line of 'Once in Royal David's City',

> When like stars his children crowned
> All in white shall wait around,

as 'one of the daftest ever written, and totally meaningless today'. The line is far from meaningless; if it is meaningless today, and to him, that clergyman should ask himself some serious questions. Should we get rid of what we do not understand? Or should we try to understand it?

The history of Israel in the Book of Dreams is divided into periods, as in Daniel, and each is in the charge of a shepherd, an angel figure. Angels, especially guardian angels, are often called shepherds in this tradition. As early as Ezekiel 34 the guardians of Israel are described as shepherds, and the pastoral imagery of Psalm 23 may mean more than we think. King David had been a shepherd, it is true, and he might naturally have chosen to describe the Lord in this way, but this must not make us overlook the other possibility. The Lord was regarded as the guardian angel of his people. This is what is meant by the name 'the Holy One of Israel'. As guardian angel he would also have been called their shepherd. There is an early Christian book called 'The Shepherd of Hermas' which was written in Rome in the middle of the second century and included in some early versions of the New Testament. It describes the visions given to Hermas by a shepherd angel who is described exactly as a shepherd, wearing a white goatskin, and carrying a shepherd's bag and staff. The first vision of the African martyr St Perpetua describes an old shepherd in white, waiting to welcome her into heaven. When Jesus says, 'I am the good shepherd', we have to remember what a shepherd represented. It did not mean just a gentle rustic figure with a lamb on his shoulders, familiar to us from our childhood Sunday School pictures. The good and bad shepherds in the apocalypses were angels. There are seventy of these angel shepherds in the Book of Dreams, and they are bad shepherds who do not care for the flock.

The history culminates with the judgement of the evil shepherds, the fallen angels and the blinded sheep, by which is meant those Israelites who have come under the influence of the fallen angels. In the code of the apocalyptists, blindness is a sign of bondage to these evil ones. This is why in John 9.1–7 Jesus cures the blind man to demonstrate the power of God, and in Matthew 23.16 he calls the Pharisees blind guides. This also explains the different ways of reading Isaiah 61.13. When Jesus read from Isaiah in the synagogue at Nazareth (Luke 4.17–19) the New Testament's account of what he read is not the same as the Old Testament version of Isaiah 61.1–3 with which we are familiar. There are several theories as to how this came about which we cannot go into here. What is important is to realize that the 'blindness' of the New Testament version is a way of describing the 'bondage' of the Old Testament version. The two readings are not really different in meaning if we place ourselves in the world of the time. This Book of Dreams, and the ideas and images in it, are very important. I shall return to it later.

The fifth section, chapters 91–104, is *The Epistle of Enoch*. The bulk of it resembles the Old Testament prophets, with threats of judgement upon sinners, and encouragement for the faithful. The form is very familiar, and immediately raises the question: 'If Enoch was quite at home in what we regard as normal prophecy, were the Old Testament prophets also at home in the world of Enoch and his angels, even though only the smallest hints of this survive in the Old Testament?' The Epistle also shows us that the theology of the Enoch writings developed over the years. In the oldest section, the Book of the Watchers, we find for example that the reward for righteousness is a prosperous old age, whereas the Epistle says that the righteous go to live among the hosts of heaven, rather like the wise of Daniel 12.3, who are promised that they will shine like the stars. It seems that this belief in life after death was a cause of great friction. Their enemies did not believe in life after death, nor did they believe in the last judgement. On the contrary, they took their present prosperity as a sign of God's favour. This suggests that the enemies of the Enochic circle were a prosperous group who had abandoned the idea of a last judgement.

When we add to this the fact that the oldest section of Enoch has no criticism of the temple, whereas the later Epistle looks to the renewal of the temple as a sign of the last days, we see that the Enoch group were not opposed to the temple worship as such, but only to the actual temple and its practices (i.e. to the second temple and what it represented). Although the early Christians came to see another meaning in the saying, Jesus claimed that he would destroy the temple and rebuild it in three days (John 2.19), a prediction, in the apocalyptist's code, for the coming of the judgement. The cleansing of the temple, which all four Gospels record as such an important event in Jesus' ministry, must also have been seen in this light. It was a declaration of judgement; the Lord had come to his temple.

Embedded within the Epistle in another account of the history of Israel, divided into periods called weeks, and known, as a result, as the Apocalypse of Weeks. There are many examples in the non-biblical books of histories written in a highly artificial form, with everything placed in a pattern of sevens or seventies. This should warn us that their idea of history writing was very different from ours. For them, history did not stop at the present, but at the last judgement, and the strange numerical patterns enabled them to see where their times were in the overall scheme. They would then know how long it would be until the Lord brought the great judgement upon their enemies. In the Apocalypse of Weeks there is a great revelation of wisdom in week seven, presumably the author's own time, after which in weeks eight, nine and ten, the righteous would triumph, the temple would be rebuilt, and the angels would be judged. In this history too we find that the three heroes are described as 'men', and that those who fell into evil ways are blind. In both the Enochic accounts of Israel's history the second temple, built after the return from Babylon, is described as impure, and its devotees as apostate.

This must suffice as the barest outline within which we shall now look at some of the ideas in 1 Enoch. In making a selection of these ideas I must necessarily be passing a judgement as to what I think is important, and since there is so much more yet to learn about these ancient texts, future generations who know them better may think this inadequate. But we must start somewhere, and in what follows I shall try to put these Enochic writings in their context, and show how their ideas have passed into Christian ways of thinking. Often these ideas have become for us no more than figures of speech – the familiar sounds of the New Testament lessons and the regular pattern of services. It is very illuminating to discover what the words once said to the first Christians.

Chapter 3

The Origin of Evil

Our ideas about the nature and cause of evil are a very important part of our ideas about religion as a whole. We cannot imagine a popular evangelist preaching without once mentioning sin, nor the Roman Catholic Church without the practice of confession. We cannot imagine Christianity without its enormous emphasis upon sin, by which we mean the sin of individual acts and attitudes, doing what we ought not to do, and not doing what we ought to do. The effect of all this emphasis upon the personal has been the neglect of the wider, we might say cosmic, side of our faith.

Christians were hard-pressed to find anything really well-rooted to say about the ecological crisis when this first became a topic of concern in the 1960s. We had no basis upon which to make suggestions, because, for better or worse, our attitudes to the creation had been coloured, whether or not we took it literally, by the story in Genesis. Man had been given the earth to master and subdue; it was his to do with as he saw fit. He had been told to multiply, and had been happy to set about this. The crisis, which came from man's domination of the earth and his zealous fulfilment of the command to breed, came as a shock. Mother earth had had enough. The New Testament gives us virtually nothing to work on for a characteristically Christian contribution to the debate. The teaching attributed to Jesus deals with birds and lilies (Matt. 6.25–9) and the value of sparrows (Matt. 10.29–31); Paul speaks about creation in language we do not understand, because we have no certain frame of reference for his ideas (Rom. 8.18–25; Col. 1.15–20).

I Enoch makes a significant contribution. It offers another account of the origin of evil, another myth to serve as the pattern for our thinking, another picture of mankind's role in the created order. Since I Enoch was known and used by the first Christians, the ideas in it may well bridge the all-too-obvious gap in the New Testament on this important matter. In addition, the world-view of I Enoch does fit very well as a background to Paul's argument in Romans 8, and this must strengthen the case for its being a long-lost piece of New Testament background material.

We are also confronted today with an increasing awareness of the occult, and this is disturbing to many Christians, especially to those whose Churches have emphasized Christian social action (a very important emphasis) and tended to neglect more supernatural matters in their efforts to communicate with the thinking people of the twentieth century. It has been supposed that 'that' side of religion is less palatable to the modern world, and so our clergy have become social workers, and our churches have continued to empty. The interest in the supernatural has been fed from elsewhere; magic is now big business, and films about the occult are guaranteed success. Popular music and lyrics have occult themes. Many people who never go near a church admit that they have had experiences which they think of as religious, because they are experiences of something irrational, something outside themselves. Some have turned to Eastern religions; often this may only take the form of Yoga. Classes are held in most village halls, though few who are drawn to practise it think of it as religious until they read of a vicar who has banned Yoga from the church hall. Many new converts to meditation have been introduced to it through the pages of *Vogue*, not by the Churches.

Within the Churches there has been a revival in the healing ministry and the ministry of exorcism. In the African Church these have created something of a crisis for the established power structures, especially the Vatican, because the gift of healing cannot be conferred and confined by the Church in the way that it regulates other offices. In a world increasingly threatened by enormous forces of evil, there has also been a grass-roots revival of ecstatic religion, a recognition of all those elements which traditional religion has tried to shut away because they cannot be institutionalized. Sociologists of religion have argued that that ecstatic religion is a form of escapism for those who find themselves powerless in society. But this only confirms my point. Those who feel themselves truly powerless in the face of great forces of evil become most painfully aware of the need for the 'other' to afford them both structure, comfort and protection in life.

How does all this relate to New Testament Christianity? It relates to it very closely indeed, if we take seriously the world-view implied in the Enochic writings, and admit the possibility that this was the world-view of the New Testament writers, and the framework within which the Christian message of salvation was first expressed. It will become apparent as we explore the Book of Enoch that our respectable established Churches have come a long way from their roots, and

34

the rediscovery of these roots may prove to be an impossibly painful business. But we cannot ignore them. I am not suggesting that Christians should return to a culture and life-style derived from first-century Palestine. What we have to do is look at the insights expressed by the strange Enochic writings, and ask if these have any relevance to the questions raised by the very different situations of the twentieth century.

It is clear to any thinking person that there is more to evil than human transgressions. There are many things evil and wrong which are not the result of human acts. There are dimensions of evil so great that we have to call them cosmic evil. Did God create evil? Or is God not all-powerful? Was there another power which formed the created order? The idea that evil in creation was the work of a lesser, hostile God was the basis of one of Christianity's earliest heresies. In the second century Marcion taught this, and his teaching was rejected by what came to be mainstream Christianity, even though he had many followers for many centuries. The question was swept under the carpet, but it did not disappear. Even now the Churches dwell upon human error and human failure, but cosmic evil is a less popular subject. We talk less about that sort of evil because ideas of evil forces at work in the creation are thought to be outgrown superstitions. If we do talk about it, it becomes a human sin to do nothing about it, not to engage in the struggle against 'it', even though 'it' is left very vague. And we still avoid the issue of why it is there in the first place.

Theologians have built elaborate structures on the subject over the centuries, but the problem remains: If we believe that God is all-good and all-powerful, and that there is only one God, why and how did evil come about? We are drawn back to the story of Adam and Eve, of human sin (by which is often meant women's sin), as the cause of all misery and necessitating our redemption. Perhaps this is because that story in Genesis is the only one we have. And yet Jesus never mentions the story, Paul makes but one reference to it, and the people of Jesus' time are known to have understood the Adam and Eve story very differently. The book of Revelation, which describes the end of evil, is clearly based on something very different from the story of the sin of Adam and Eve. Despite all this, that story has dominated the ideas we have come to think of as Christian.

The opening words of the old baptism service emphasized this: 'forasmuch as all men are conceived and born in sin . . .' How often too have we heard someone in a moment of anger or despair say,

'What have I done to deserve this?' How many people who come apart and need expert help are the victims of their own religious system, destroyed by the feelings of guilt, inadequacy and dependence which have been implanted by a religious upbringing? In women this is particularly so, as their status in society has for so long been determined by the 'Christian view' of their proper role. If we are honest, they are more often victims who need protection than evil ones who need to repent. The biblical view of the remedy for 'sin' seems to be more one of healing a wound than of punishing a wrong. What has been broken has to be made whole, not further fragmented.

There is good reason to believe that sin and evil in Jesus' time were explained very differently. Of course they did not have the same issues to face as we do today, but the fundamental issue of cosmic evil is one of which they were all too well aware. They gave an important place to the role of evil angels and the forces of Satan. They had a picture of a vast conspiracy of evil actively engaged in a struggle against humankind, working to corrupt and destroy the creation. People needed protection against this onslaught, and help to overcome its effects. They were not hampered by our sophisticated attitudes, which have come to terms with evil forces by saying that they do not exist, or by turning them into a form of late-night entertainment. Our Christian ancestors in the time of Jesus would have recognized this ploy. The devil, they knew, acted through the human mind, where man was most proud and therefore most vulnerable. To convince a thinking man that evil forces did not exist was indeed a triumph.

In order to reconstruct this other view of the world, let us start with the last book of the New Testament, which is also the last chapter of the early Christian world-view. It describes the conflict of the faithful with Satan and other evil powers, and the reward for those who endure and fight alongside the good powers. (This is what lies behind Rev. 14.4. The virtue of celibacy was that you lived like a good angel. The evil angels had fallen through their lust.) Beast and dragon are destroyed, Satan is bound in a great pit, and finally there is a new heaven and a new earth. This is the same pattern as we find in Enoch, where the oppressed righteous are rescued by archangels from the fearful influence and power of the fallen angels. Asael is imprisoned in a pit in the desert, and the earth then enjoys fertility, prosperity and peace. This picture has only the remotest link to the Adam and Eve story, where an evil creature caused humankind to go astray and hanker after the divine knowledge which had been forbidden to them.

As a result of human disobedience the earth became a place of dust and thistles. The Book of Revelation, then, seems to be the last chapter of the Enochic story of evil, and not to be derived from the story in Genesis.

When we look at the Old Testament, we discover that Adam and Eve are simply not mentioned anywhere except in Genesis 2–3. Now if the Adam and Eve story had been the explanation of sin, we should have expected at least some reference to it. The most likely explanation is that the story was added to the Old Testament at a very late stage in its compilation, and placed as a preface to the whole work, which in many places has a very different view of the nature of sin and evil. The Adam and Eve story in Genesis says that human disobedience is the cause of evil; we have also read into it the later idea of inheriting Adam's sin, even though this is not a biblical idea. When the Adam and Eve story was used by later Jewish writers, it was used like a parable to describe the individual experience of every human being who had separated himself from God by wilful disobedience. It did not describe the downfall of the whole race and the inherited horror of original sin.

In the New Testament we find two views of evil side by side. Jesus not only forgives sins caused by disobedience to the Law; he also engages in a conflict with evil powers and heals people. If you read just the first three chapters of Mark's Gospel, a clear relationship between these two different aspects emerges: exorcism at Capernaum (1.23–26); healing Simon's mother-in-law (1.30–31); the gathering of the sick and demon-possessed (1.32–34); the leper (1.40–42); the paralytic whose sins were forgiven (2.3–12); the man with the withered hand (3.1–5); the Jerusalem scribes accusing Jesus of being an agent of Satan (3.22–30). Conflict with evil was a vital part of the healing process, whether these evils were caused by personal failure or demonic influence. We have until recently tended to neglect the healing ministry, seeing it best handled by conventional Western medicine; medicine and religion have been separated to their mutual impoverishment. The business of exorcism and demon-possession has been kept even more closely under wraps, despite the fact that Jesus' command to his disciples was to cast out demons and teach. Perhaps the recovery of an ancient and more integrated world-view will help us to recover some of the original insight and impact of Jesus' teaching, and to appreciate what we can learn from new Christians of the Third World, who can relate more directly to this ministry of

Jesus. We see the beginnings of reintegration in the trend towards treating the whole person, not just the physical manifestations of illness – a hopeful sign that we are recovering an awareness of the invisible world.

Enoch spells out in detail another picture of the origin of evil. (I do not say 'the other account', since there were several versions.) Enoch describes the fall of the angels. There was a major rift in the heavens, and what had been created good became distorted and corrupt through pride and self-will. As I said in the last chapter, there are at least two strands interwoven in Enoch, and there is another which we can read between the lines in the Old Testament. Enoch describes how Asael, a powerful angel who knew the secrets of the creation, came to earth and taught humankind some of those secrets. This heavenly knowledge gave men godlike powers, and thus they corrupted the earth. They learnt how to extract metals from rock, and to use them to make weapons of war and ornaments for seduction. (A later version of this story says that it was the beautifully adorned women who lured still more angels to the earth.) Enoch also describes how two hundred angels, led by Semihazah, looked down from heaven and saw the beautiful daughters of men. They lusted for them, and came to earth to rape them and father half-breed children who were monsters and demons. In later 'wisdom' writings we see that knowledge/wisdom was regarded as the feminine or creative aspect of God. Proverbs 8 shows one example of this idea; clearer though less well known is Wisdom of Solomon 7.21–22, 25:

> I learned both what is secret and what is manifest,
> for wisdom, the fashioner of all things, taught me . . .
>
> For she is a breath of the power of God,
> and a pure emanation of the glory of the Almighty;
> therefore nothing defiled gains entrance into her.

Here in 1 Enoch we find the much older mythological expression of the same idea. Heavenly beings revolt against the divine order, take divine wisdom for their own ends, and this results in the abuse of women and the corruption of creation. Despite its bizarre expression, the insight is profound. The urge to power shows itself in the abuse of wisdom, which is the feminine, creative aspect of God, and this manifests itself on earth in an exactly parallel form, the abuse of women and the corruption of the creation. In Hebrew the verb 'know' covered both knowledge and sexual activity. (The latter is used at e.g. Gen. 4.1: 'Adam knew Eve his wife, and she conceived . . .') The association was deep-rooted. In fact the two were aspects of the one corruption; those who aspired to be gods had to gain control of the creative processes. (This pattern is remarkably relevant to some of the unacknowledged problems facing the priesthood today. Those priests who see their role as that of the visible representative and representation of Christ and who argue that this must exclude women from the priesthood, are actually taking for themselves the role of gods. This 'high' view of the priesthood also involves them in a creative role which is essentially feminine in its imagery. They alone can break the body which gives life, they alone feed the faithful, even though the life-giving and feeding roles are essentially feminine ones. Without a monopoly of the creative, feminine role, there would be no power left to them. Now, as then, it is a corruption.) In Enoch's myth one group chose to destroy the creation by assuming the role of gods. The souls of those destroyed by the incursion of evil brought their pleas to the gate of heaven, and God ordered the archangels to enter the conflict on behalf of the oppressed, to bind the evil angels, and prepare for the great judgement.

Semihazah's angels did not only father half-breed children; they also taught them the heavenly secrets which gave them power to oppress human beings. There are several versions of what these secrets were, but they show us the areas of life in which people felt most threatened by evil. One version says that they were metalworking and manufacture of weapons, medicine and enchantments (in those days very similar), astrology and various signs for reading the future. Another says they taught about weapons, medicine, writing, demons and abortions. A third says they taught sorcery, witchcraft, metallurgy and the making of images. One of the non-biblical books from the second century BC, Jubilees, describes how Noah was taught medicine by the good angels in order to counteract the effects of the evil ones. This shows us that the knowledge brought by the fallen ones was not thought of as bad in itself, but bad when used apart from the laws of God. Medicine could be used for good or ill. Metalworking, writing, exorcism, even reading the future, were similarly evil when placed in the wrong hands, because they were the key to great power.

There is also a third version of the angel myth itself which describes the sin of pride. Any angel who forgot his true place in the created order and attempted to set himself up as a god was thrown from heaven. This pride was described in different ways; the proud angel might try to climb too high on the mountain of God, in order to set himself over the great throne; or he might take it upon himself to use his wisdom for his own glory. Thus in Isaiah 14 we find the proud star/king of Babylon who set his throne higher than God himself, and Ezekiel 28 describes the angel/king of Tyre who abused his wisdom: 'In the abundance of your trade you were filled with violence, and you sinned' (Ezek. 28.16).

The early Christians were not the first to apply these myths to their own situation. They were not ancient tales which suddenly took on a new significance. We must read these stories about angels as the source of a lively tradition of theology, the framework within which life could be interpreted. Even within the Enochic writings we have evidence that they were being used as the basis for comment on contemporary situations. The angels who lusted and took earthly wives, for example, are thought to have been used as the pattern for condemning the corrupted priesthood of the second century BC. There was already a relationship between priests and angels in their way of thinking, so this application of the angel myth would have been quite natural. They believed that the temple represented heaven on earth, and the priests were those who functioned in the heavenly rituals of the temple. The counterpart of the earthly temple was the heavenly reality, also a great temple, where angels were ministers before the throne of God. One of the most beautiful of the texts found at Qumran is a collection of hymns which describe vividly how the angels ministered in the heavenly temple, clad in priestly vestments, and mirroring in every way the cult as it was practised in Jerusalem (*The Songs of the Sabbath Sacrifice* 4Q ShirShabb). (It is this picture of the two temples which lies behind the complicated parallelism of Hebrews 9.)

Others saw in the story of the fallen angels the political struggles of their time between the heirs of Alexander the Great. The Ptolemies of Egypt and the Seleucids of Syria disputed the possession of Palestine throughout the third century BC, and the evil angels who caused the bloodshed were seen at work in the political leaders of the day. We see an exactly similar picture in Daniel, where angel princes fight the heavenly counterpart of contemporary earthly battles (Dan. 10. 12–14), and the threat to the temple mount in Jerusalem from the mad Seleucid king Antiochus Epiphanes is seen as a threat from a proud heavenly figure attempting to climb the mountain of God by entering his sanctuary (Dan. 8.10–12). A similar story was told of the haughty Assyrian general who threatened Jerusalem in the time of Hezekiah (Isa. 37). Isaiah was able to assure the king that because the general had come in pride against the Holy One of Israel, he was doomed (Isa. 37.22–29). This way of interpreting history in terms of the angels was very deeply rooted in Israel's traditions; it seems very strange to us because we have always read the stories in our own way. Their very familiarity has prevented our understanding them.

Other parts of the Enochic writings use other parts of the myth. The two versions of Israel's history in the Book of Dreams and the Epistle give a prominent role to angels, and forsaking wisdom is seen as a major cause of disaster. The Old Testament account is different; the disaster of the fall of Jerusalem was caused by forsaking the Law of Moses, not by forsaking wisdom. Here we see clearly the two traditions; law, which became the Old Testament tradition as we know it, and wisdom, which survived outside the Old Testament, and in Christianity. The whole of life was governed by the angel powers, even to the most mundane details. The Similitudes tell of an evil ruler (Herod?) who had built himself a residence by the Dead Sea, to enjoy the thermal springs. The weird landscape of these parts has given them many associations with the scene of the last judgement, and the writer wryly comments that the evil king will soon be heating his bathwater, along with the other burning angels beneath the valley!

It was in a world peopled with such angels that Christianity had its roots. The very names that the Christians gave themselves show how closely they identified with the world of the angels. They called themselves 'sons of God' (Rom. 8.14, cf. Gen. 6.1–2, where the sons of Gods are the angels who marry the daughters of men), and they called themselves the 'saints', (Eph. 1.1; Phil. 1.1; Col. 1.2, etc), a name which actually means 'holy ones', members of the heavenly host. Hebrews 12.22 describes Christians in the angelic gathering in the heavenly Jerusalem. At the heart of the Eucharist we still say:

> Therefore with Angels and Archangels,
> and with all the company of heaven,
> we laud and magnify thy glorious Name,
> evermore praising thee and saying:
> Holy, holy, holy, Lord God of hosts,
> heaven and earth are full of thy glory:
> Glory be to thee, O Lord most High.

This is drawn from the song of the angels in Isaiah (Isa. 6.3), and in Enoch (1 Enoch 39.12).

We find allusions to this lost mythology throughout the New Testament; some are very clear, others now seem rather trivial. The command in 1 Corinthians 11.10 that women should wear hats in church is based on a fear of the angels. Why? When the sons of God looked down from heaven and saw the daughters of men, they would have seen their beautiful hair. To avoid any further disasters, women had to keep their hair covered! (Notice the characteristic stance of Paul: the very existence of the woman's beauty invites disaster, and she has to do something about it. We see a similar attitude in modern sentencing for rape, where it has been suggested that women who do not observe a curfew deserve what comes to them. Alas, this is a traditional Christian attitude.)

The angels also shed light on the nativity stories, as we should expect, since angels feature throughout. In a rewriting of Genesis found at Qumran (the Genesis Apocryphon) the story is told of the birth of Noah. He was such a remarkable child, and so unlike his father, that his mother was suspected of having conceived him from an angel. She had to assure the family that Noah was a natural child. We have often been told that the people of Jesus' time would have found the idea of a divine child quite scandalous, just a pagan nonsense and quite out of keeping with the strict Jewish belief in one God. Yet here at Qumran, in a community of very pious and conservative people who had rejected the worldliness of the Jerusalem temple, we find the story of an angel child. We are bound to be reminded of the story of the annunciation, and the promise to Mary that her child would be a son of the Most High God.

This belief in angel and demon children goes right through the New Testament. The demons whom Jesus expels are the interesting offspring of Semihazah's angels, and they recognize Jesus as the son of the Most High God, the one they know will defeat them. The corrupting knowledge of Asael is what lies beneath Romans 8, where Paul describes a creation in bondage to decay, waiting to be set free with the coming of the sons of God. Christians were the new generation of the sons of God, working with God to renew and restore the creation, reversing the process begun by the fallen ones. Thus would be achieved the happy state described in the very earliest Enochic theology, a world of fertility, prosperity and peace. The angels who sinned through pride and tried to set themselves up as gods are the key to understanding Philippians 2.5–11, where Jesus is contrasted with those who wanted equality with God. He was exalted because of his humility. He did not try to take equality with God for himself.

The conflict with evil was not simply exorcism, but also healing. We tend to think of them separately, but in New Testament times they were aspects of one healing process. There was, for example, a relationship between the words blind, lame, deaf and dumb and the names for the various categories of evil angels. We do not know exactly how this relationship worked, but in each case the Hebrew name for the angel is similar to that for the affliction. Thus 'Watcher' in Hebrew is the name for an evil angel, but it is also very like the word for blind. We know from Enoch's Book of Dreams that people under the power of the Watchers became blind. Jesus' healing of blindness was a sign that the power was broken. Other angel names corresponded to lame, deaf and dumb. When we consider what a large number of Jesus' healing miracles were concerned with just these afflictions, we realize that there was more to the conflict with evil than straightforward exorcism. This evil showed itself in physical disabilities.

The New Testament is so familiar to us that we can easily miss this all-pervasive world of angels. Look at the angel elements in Matthew's Gospel, for example. We have wise men and a star, Joseph warned by angels in a dream, the conflict with Satan in the temptation story, healing and exorcizing throughout the Gospel, the command to love enemies and so be sons of the Father (i.e. like angels), Capernaum brought to Hades on the day of judgement (like the fallen cities whose guardian angels had been cast out), the secrets of the Kingdom of Heaven, the angel reapers of the last judgement, the righteous shining like the sun (i.e. exalted to heaven and transformed), blind guides, the power to bind and loose in heaven and on earth (see chapter 6), little ones with guardian angels in heaven, cleansing the temple (the earthly counterpart of heaven and the scene of the Judgement), the question about divorce with the answer that angels do not marry, the apocalyptic predictions of the fate of Jerusalem and the coming of the Son of Man, and the angel at the tomb on Easter morning. Everywhere there are angels, or ideas which we now know are associated with them. We cannot possibly read this Gospel without taking the angelic setting into account.

The most vivid point of contact with the Enochic tradition is the parable in Matthew 25, where the sheep and the goats gather before the great throne, awaiting sentence. The evil ones go to the fire which has been prepared for the devil and his angels (Matt. 25.41). In 1 Enoch 90.20–27 we also read of a judgement before the great throne. Those awaiting judgement are described as sheep (all the human beings in this section are depicted as animals), and they are condemned to the fiery abyss, along with the seventy wicked shepherd angels.

In other places our emphasis upon a great sacrifice for our personal sins has led us to overlook the equally important picture of a sacrifice to protect us from threatening evil. A sacrifice for personal sins belongs to the world of the Law and personal responsibility for our actions, whereas a sacrifice to afford protection belongs to a world of threatening evil. The earliest Christians were all too well aware of the evil all around them. In 1 Corinthians 5.7 we find an early Christian hymn which describes Christ as the Passover lamb which has been sacrificed. The Fourth Gospel implies the same thing; Jesus was killed at the time when the Passover lambs were killed (John 19.14,31). Now the Passover sacrifice symbolized many things: release from slavery, or the beginning of a new life as the people of God; but as originally described in Exodus 12, the blood of the Passover lamb protected people from the angel of death. The first Christians saw the death of Jesus as a protection against the ever-threatening powers of evil, whose ultimate triumph was corruption and death. Thus Colossians 2.15 says that on the cross Christ overcame the threatening powers of the universe; he overcame death. The whole of this chapter in Colossians deals with the cult of the angels, and the threat that this posed to Christianity. The almost incomprehensible argument in Hebrews 1 is also based on beliefs about Christ being greater than the angels, although exactly what these beliefs and arguments were we can no longer tell. 1 Peter 3.22 says that the powers of heaven have been subjected to Jesus, as does Philippians 2.5–11. 1 John 3.8 says that the Son of God came to destroy the work of the devil.

The angelic judgement was expected to happen in the near future. The Qumran writings are full of references to the great struggle which was to precede the End of this Age and the establishment of God's rule on earth, and the community there lived in a state of ritual purity, awaiting the summons to battle. Current events were interpreted as the preliminaries. They described themselves as the sons of light, battling against the sons of darkness, and one of their texts, the War

Scroll, shows how literally they believed the forces of evil to be involved with the politics of their day. When the battle came it would be a real earthly battle, but squadrons of angels were expected to augment the army of the sons of light, and allowance was made for this in their plans. The battle against the powers of darkness involved them in the political struggles of their day. The earliest Christian belief was that the judgement would happen within the lifetime of the first generation, but as the years passed the belief was modified. 2 Thessalonians 1.7 shows this early expectation, with the prediction that Jesus would come from heaven with fiery angels. 2 Thessalonians 2.4 describes a proud one who exalts himself above God, a reference to the angel myth. 2 Peter 2 is full of this angel imagery, as are Jude and Revelation.

But how does this battle against evil in all its forms relate to the role of the Messiah? As with so many other familiar words in the New Testament, we have tended to give 'Messiah' our own meaning, often forgetting that Jesus was called Messiah because the people of his time knew what they meant by a Messiah. The Christian teaching modified the traditional view, but it was only a modification, not a completely new departure. Messiah, and its Greek equivalent Christ, means the 'anointed one'. In Jesus' time the people's expectations of the Messiah were built upon the memories of the ancient kings of Jerusalem, albeit much elaborated by centuries of frustrated nationalism and prophetic fervour. These ancient kings of Israel were very different from our idea of a king, and the Old Testament has obscured many aspects of the ancient monarchy. The texts most influenced by the Deuteronomists (those who compiled Deuteronomy and several other Old Testament books) give a very 'unangelic' picture of the kings, but in older texts we can see that the king had been seen as a semi-divine figure, with titles such as 'Son of God', and 'Servant of the Lord'. He was the great mediator between his people and God, and he also spoke as the servant and mouthpiece of God. Several psalms show us this exalted role (e.g. Pss. 2 and 110). Others (e.g. Ps. 72) show how the good king was the source not only of justice but also of fertility and prosperity. Psalm 89 depicts the king on earth reflecting the power and role of God in heaven. As God ruled the powers of the heavens, and commanded the waters of the sea, so his earthly agent ruled the powers of the earth and commanded the seas (cf. Mark 4.41: 'Who then is this, that even wind and sea obey him?').

The Old Testament tells us surprisingly little about the ancient kings, and nothing at all about their laws, but we have another source of information in the historian Josephus, who was a younger contemporary of Jesus. He wrote a history of the Jewish people which was based on the Old Testament but supplemented with a great deal of other material. Some of it may have been of dubious value, but he does give some interesting information about the kings. Whether or not his history was strictly accurate, it at least shows us what the people of Jesus' time thought the kings had been like, and presumably what they expected a king and Messiah to be. Solomon, he tells us, was a healer and an exorcist who passed on his skills to his successors (Antiquities 8.45). Solomon was the son of David, and there are those who think that 'Son of David' was a title later given to those with healing gifts. Solomon's power over demons was to become legendary. Magical texts were published in his name, and even as late as the Arabian Nights we find the tale of the Poor Fisherman who found a copper vase sealed with the seal of Solomon. When he opened it a fearful genie emerged, who said he had been imprisoned by Solomon for refusing to acknowledge his authority. He had been sealed into the vase with a great seal of lead which bore the sacred name of God. The kings of Israel were remembered as sons of God, exorcists and healers, the front line of the battle against the fallen ones who threatened the people of God. It is this aspect of the messianic hope which we find in Luke 11.20: 'If it is by the finger of God that I cast out demons, then the kingdom of God has come upon you.' The presence of the agent of God was proof that the kingdom (i.e. the power) of God was there. For the first three centuries many Christians thought of Jesus as an angel figure, leading the great battle against evil. The Shepherd of Hermas describes Jesus as a holy and venerable angel. The Ebionites, one of the groups within Jewish Christianity, said that Christ had been created like the archangels, but greater.

The evil of the fallen angels took many forms; demon-possession and illness were but two of them, the work of their half-breed children. The work of the Messiah and his successors, the new sons of God, was to heal and exorcize. This struggle against demons was to become the basis of later monastic life, especially in Egypt, where extreme asceticism was thought to be the best weapon with which to fight the angelic battle. But the greatest work of evil was the corruption of wisdom, and it is here that this bizarre mythology begins to show its abiding relevance. Wisdom in itself was neutral, but those who possessed it acquired godlike powers, and it was necessary above all that the wise should fear God and obey his laws. There is much dispute about wisdom in the Old Testament. We know that angels were wise, that Adam and Eve were tempted by the serpent who promised them they would be like gods (or God, the Hebrew can mean either) if they gained knowledge. We know that the angel king of Tyre abused his wisdom (Ezek. 28) and was thrown from the presence of God. All these examples show the effect of wisdom, but exactly what wisdom was is less easy to say. Unfortunately the Old Testament does not answer all the questions we should like to put to it, and we have to do the best we can with what we have. The classic definition of wisdom is that of the opening verses of the book of Proverbs, but even this does not tell us what the learning and skills actually comprised. Job 28 takes us a little further. In describing the things which are not true wisdom (which for the poet is the fear of the Lord), we have some clues as to what others believed wisdom to be. It was mining and engineering skill, perhaps commerce too. The wisdom of the king of Tyre was certainly shown as commercial skill, a skill which he abused. The wisdom of the evil angels in Enoch's account was the knowledge of medicine, production of metals used to make weapons, knowledge of writing, knowledge of magic, the control of men's minds and actions.

The fallen angels could manifest themselves in their earthly agents, the blind, or in political leaders as 'the angels of the nations'. They had power because they were wise. The wise men who were also thought to have access to the heavenly knowledge were advisers to kings. They interpreted men's dreams for them and told them what their future would be. In other words, they were the shapers of ideas, as well as the possessors of knowledge. All this, says the theology of Enoch, was corrupted when the evil angels chose to corrupt the created order and to set themselves up as gods. It is small wonder that the Old Testament's most frequent comment on wisdom is that the fear of the Lord is the beginning of wisdom. The Messiah was expected to fight against, and to protect his people from, these threatening evils. But if Christians are also called to be sons of God, we can see the logic of Paul's argument in Romans 8. The whole corrupted and suffering creation was waiting for the new sons of God to release it from the bondage to evil, not just from physical evil, but from every abuse of its secrets.

This cosmic aspect of the battle means looking at modern manifestations of wisdom and knowledge (and they are surprisingly like

Enoch's), and guarding against their corruption by wise men who think they are gods. We must look at commercial and industrial practices, medicine, the making of weapons, the many facets of communication (writing), and shaping opinions (interpreting dreams) and the abuse of women (taking the daughters of men). Above all, we must look at political leaders, and the wise men who advise them. Fallen angels, unchecked gods, can still oppress and corrupt the creation. 1 Enoch 9.10 is as relevant today as it ever was: 'And now, behold, the souls of those who have died are crying and making their suit to the gates of heaven, and their lamentations have ascended'; as is the hope expressed in 10.18, 11.1: 'then shall the whole earth be tilled in righteousness, and shall all be planted with trees and be full of blessing . . . And in those days I will open the store chambers of blessing which are in the heaven, so as to send them down upon the earth over the work and labour of the children of men.'

The mythology of the angels, like all myths, survived because it worked as a pattern for interpreting life. It still carries a fundamental insight we might well consider bringing back to our reading of the New Testament.

Chapter 4

The Vision of God

In the Book of the Watchers, Enoch ascends to heaven, sees the great throne of God, and then travels through the heavens observing their secrets. The description in these chapters has caused a radical reassessment of the religious scene in the pre-Christian centuries. There is no doubt that the chapters describe a mystical ascent; they are related to the later mystical texts which describe the contemplation of the great chariot throne of God. Nobody had suspected that these mystical practices were so ancient.

In 1 Enoch 14 we are told that Enoch is carried up to heaven with clouds, mists and winds. He sees a crystal wall surrounded by fire, and then a crystal house with stars and lightning as its ceiling, and fiery cherubim. Within this house was a second house of fire, and in this there was a crystal throne with shining wheels, and more cherubim. Streams of fire flowed from under the throne, and on it was the Great Glory in shining white robes. Ten thousand times ten thousand angels stood before him. One of the holy ones told Enoch to enter. The Great Glory told him to take a message of judgement to the Watchers who had left heaven to take human wives, and had thus lost their angelic status and their eternal life.

Enoch is then taken on a heavenly journey to see the treasuries of the stars, the source of the lightning, the mouths of the rivers and deeps. He sees the foundations of the earth, and the winds which blow and cause the stars to move. He sees six fabulous mountains of jewels, surrounding the mountain of the throne of God, which has a sapphire summit. He sees the fiery abyss, and the burning mountains which are evil angels, and he is told the names and duties of the seven archangels. On a second journey Enoch sees the chaos of darkness and the prison of the angels; he sees the three smooth places where the souls of men assemble for judgement, divided according to whether or not they have received their just deserts on earth. He sees the Tree of Life waiting to be returned to the Holy Place in Jerusalem, and he sees mountains and valleys, plantations of fragrant trees and the doors through which the winds blow various weathers.

This curious experience of ascent is one which is found in many cultures, both ancient and modern, and although some writers used the ascent and revelation pattern as nothing more than a pious fiction, for most it has been the record of a genuine experience. The outer edges of the human mind are still waiting to be explored, and experiences similar to the ascent of Enoch have been described by people under the influence of certain drugs. We know that the experiences can be induced in several ways, of which fasting is the commonest. It would be very interesting to know what Ezra was eating at 2 Esdras 12.31; in order to prepare himself for visions he sat in a field and ate only flowers and plants. What is important is not the raw experience in itself, but the way in which it has been interpreted. The myth of the angels here in the Enochic vision becomes the means of interpreting and controlling the abnormal experience, and the experience itself serves to reinforce the view that the mythology is correct. Visions were fundamental to the Enochic circle, and they were fundamental in early Christianity. Several of the ideas generated by these visions, or perhaps confirmed by them, appear in the New Testament.

The origin of Enoch's type of throne vision lies far back in the Old Testament, but there is good reason to believe that the visionaries were out of favour with those who compiled the final form of much of the Old Testament. We see only glimpses of something behind the present Old Testament text. At this point those who are unfamiliar with the world of biblical scholarship may well pause. We tend not to think of the Old Testament as 'compiled, edited or censored', but it was. It is all a matter of the words we choose to describe the process. What we must not do is imagine that the Old Testament originated like the Qu'rān or the Book of Mormon. It was not revealed word for word in its final form. The process of altering and reinterpreting Scripture has always gone on. At some point a line was drawn, and the 'holy' texts were set apart. Commentaries continued to be written, but were labelled as such and separately shelved. The Book of Jubilees, which has also been found at Qumran, shows us an earlier stage of this process of adapting Scripture. It is a complete rewriting of Genesis in order to incorporate into the sacred text the views of the author. In his revised version of Genesis, the Law of Moses was known and observed even before Moses himself. Abraham, Isaac and Jacob were bound by the sacred calendar and offered correct sacrifices. The writer's motives were doubtless the very highest; for him the Law of Moses was eternal and governed everything. Many must have thought him inspired, or his work would not have survived, yet he clearly rewrote Genesis.

We must not allow ourselves to be shocked by this attitude to Scripture. The practice still continues, although under another name. Whenever we try to make Scripture relevant for today, we do the same thing as did the writer of the Book of Jubilees. Many of those who expound Scripture actually read their own views into it, and take great comfort from finding that the Scripture agrees with them. It has only been the advent of feminism, with its totally different and sometimes strange readings of Scripture, which has made us aware that accepted 'authentic' readings are often equally strange and conditioned by the interpreter. But, says an anxious voice, at least they did not rewrite the Scriptures. They did. The spate of modern English translations, and the differences between them, show that where there was obscurity or difficulty, the translator used his own judgement. If there were not differences between them, why were so many versions necessary? Perhaps there was a feeling that the other modern versions had not yet expressed the exact sense of Scripture.

If we now return to Enoch's vision, whose antecedents have disappeared from the Old Testament, we must ask ourselves: 'If the author of the Book of Jubilees rewrote Genesis in order to incorporate his own inspiration, what was rewritten to give us Genesis, and what was the new insight of that author?' Scholars often talk about sources and editors when dealing with the composition of Genesis, without addressing the question of whether or not the unedited materials might have survived elsewhere. 'Sources and editors' or 'old traditions and censors' – it just comes down to a matter of words, and the point of view one wishes to adopt. Those who were suspicious of the visionaries were those who eventually decided the form of the Old Testament.

In Exodus 24.9–11 there is an account of how Moses received the Law on Sinai. He saw the God of Israel and he saw the sapphire pavement beneath the throne. This chapter is confused, but we seem to have an account of Moses being summoned up the mountain of God into the actual presence of God. Isaiah also saw the Lord on the throne, surrounded by angels, when he was called to be a prophet (Isa. 6) and, like Enoch, to take a message of judgement. In his vision the throne of God is in the temple. Ezekiel saw the great chariot throne with all its heavenly creatures, when he was called and told to take

God's message to a 'rebellious house' (Ezek. 1;10). Isaiah and Ezekiel had similar experiences – the presence of the great throne, and the commission to be God's agent, bringing the message of judgement. It is clear that Enoch stands in the same tradition, as does the seer John. Revelation describes how the latter was caught up to heaven, and saw the great throne. He was commissioned to take messages to the seven churches, and he was shown the secrets of the judgement.

In complete contrast we have the teaching of Deuteronomy, which emphasizes very strongly that the Lord was not seen when the Law was given. Deuteronomy 4.12 says that only a voice was heard, cf. Exodus 33.18–23, where Moses asks to see the glory of God and is told that nobody can see God and live. Now the Deuteronomists played an important part in collecting and transmitting the Old Testament texts, and it would seem that they were opposed to some of the traditions in Isaiah, Ezekiel, Enoch and, later, Revelation. This may mean that the type of Jewish religion in which Christianity had its roots was seen by some Jews as heretical even before the time of Jesus. One of the crucial issues was the vision of God; was it possible, and what did it mean? When we examine the ideas associated with the vision of God we realize how fundamental it was.

Isaiah and Ezekiel show us that the vision was a very ancient practice, yet when Enoch was discovered among the Dead Sea Scrolls, and scholars realized that ascent visions were part of the religion of the third century BC, this came as a surprise. The visions of Isaiah and Ezekiel had not been thought of in that way, and maybe the way these prophetic books have been read has been heavily influenced by the tendency to suppress the visionaries. It was against the Jewish Law to read the chariot chapters of Ezekiel when one was young and unsupervised. They were considered dangerous. Why? Now that we have the Enochic material, we have to change all our pictures of the religious beliefs and practices in Palestine, and alter what we see as the background to the New Testament.

There is also pressure from another quarter to alter our ideas about the background to the New Testament. Much of the material which has been used to reconstruct the religion of Jesus' time has been derived from the writings of the later rabbis; yet in some cases they were centuries later. The written evidence for the earlier religion of Palestine was salvaged and collected after the Roman destruction of Jerusalem in AD 70 and we do not know how it was decided what to keep, or who made the decisions. We have, in fact, a very biased picture, which is almost certainly inaccurate and could be very far out indeed, yet we have tried to reconstruct the background of the New Testament on this basis. We have no real evidence about the Sadducees (i.e. none of their own works), nor have we anything about the Essenes in the writings of the rabbis. Why is there this silence? One of the consequences of our having only a part of the picture, but treating it as though it were the whole, has been the suggestion that a great deal of the New Testament ideas must have been influenced by pagan Greek thought, because there was nothing like them in the Jewish writings that survived. Even the central teaching of Jesus as the Redeemer has been said to come from another religion. Now that our picture of Judaism at that time is becoming clearer, almost everything in the New Testament can be seen to stem from Palestine. We may soon be able to place all of it in its proper setting. And the discovery of Enoch's throne vision has been a major reason for making these alterations.

When Enoch ascends to the heavenly places, he not only receives the message of judgement, he also learns the secrets of the creation. This association of the vision of God and scientific knowledge (what seems strange to us was science to them) is very important, not because the scientific knowledge is in any way accurate, but because it is entrusted to those who have a special calling into the presence of God. Knowledge of the workings of creation is part of the vision of God. There are many other accounts of revelations apart from these in Enoch, and from these other texts we can see that there was a wide interest in scientific matters. Clues as to the breadth of these interests come from the list of knowledge which the fallen angels taught, and the best example of the form the knowledge took is the Enochic Astronomy Book, which does not list the result of experimental observations, but states the nature of astronomy as an angelic revelation.

We find an interesting confirmation of this association of trance states and scientific knowledge in the reports of anthropologists who have studied shamans and witch doctors. Many claim that the traditional medicines and cures used by their people were revealed to them or their ancestors when they were in a trance. (Another curious parallel may be drawn from the writing of the Protestant mystic Jacob Boehme (1575–1624), who as a result of his experience of the presence of God felt that he had had revealed to him more than if he had been many years at a university.)

In order to see how this knowledge of the creation and revelation of judgement fit together in their natural setting, we have to find where the ascent visions began in Israel's history. It was not with the prophets, but with the kings of Jerusalem, the anointed ones, and we have to piece this together from the clues that are left to us. Psalm 89.19 is obscure, but it does link together vision, exaltation (i.e. ascent) and coronation: 'Of old thou didst speak in a vision to thy faithful one, and say: "I have set the crown upon one who is mighty, I have exalted one chosen from the people . . ." ' I Kings 3 says that Solomon was given wisdom by God in a dream. Psalm 2, a coronation psalm, says that the king was made a son of God, and set on Zion, the holy hill. We used to assume that this merely meant being established in Jerusalem, but in the light of the Enoch tradition it may mean that the king was set as a son of God, an angel figure, on the mountain of God which we know was represented by Zion. We also know from Ezekiel 28 that the mountain of God was a garden of trees and cherubim, where there were wise angel figures. Ezekiel tells us of only one, the angel/king of Tyre who was thrown down because he abused his wisdom. If the king of Tyre was a wise creature who walked on the holy mountain in the presence of God, perhaps the king of Jerusalem was similar. The anointed one was wise and was able to ascend to the presence of God, the heavenly Garden of Eden. But all this has been overlaid in the Old Testament as we now have it. We can still see that the ruler of Jerusalem was wise, with knowledge of the creation (Solomon uttered three thousand wise sayings, and these were about the natural order, I Kings 4.32–33). It makes a great deal of difference to our picture of the Messiah in the New Testament, if the name had formerly meant the anointed one who enjoyed the presence of God and had the status of an angel. In the pattern beginning to emerge, the vision of God was linked to knowledge, to the judgement, to ascent, and to angelic status, and all these were linked to the anointed one. All these also come through as a pattern in early Christian thought.

The ascent visions were associated with the temple and its rituals. Psalm 11 shows how the temple was thought to be the place of the heavenly throne, the throne which Isaiah saw. Ezekiel saw the chariot throne move out of the temple (Ezek. 10), to be with the exiles in Babylon (Ezek. 1.1–3). Enoch's vision describes the temple: one house within another house, and the throne of God within that inner house. John sees in his vision the golden lampstand (Rev. 1.12), the throne (4.2), bowls of incense (5.8), the altar (6.9). He was also in a temple setting. As early as Psalm 73.17 the judgement had been associated with the temple. The judgement on the king of Tyre, however, did not take place in what is called the temple, but in the heavenly Garden of Eden on the mountain of God. This was not a separate tradition about the judgement, but one of the surviving clues we have that the temple represented the heavenly Garden of Eden. Again we have to reconstruct as best we can. In his vision of the temple, Ezekiel sees a building on a high mountain (40.2), decorated with trees and cherubim (41.17–18), and from it flows a great river (47.1–12) which brings wonderful fertility. Later legends and traditions suggest that the temple's seven-branched candlestick represented both the Tree of Life from the Garden of Eden, and also the presence of God in the temple. There is a hint of this in Zechariah 4, a very muddled chapter (it should be read vv. 1–5, then vv. 10b–14). In that vision of Zechariah there is a seven-branched candlestick with a tree on either side. The angel tells Zechariah that the two trees represent two anointed ones standing by the Lord. The Lord must be represented by the candlestick, and the anointed ones must stand in his presence. Revelation also takes up these temple features, and the river of the water of life described in chapter 22 is exactly that of Ezekiel's vision.

The best-known of the Old Testament visions of judgement is Daniel 7, which became such an important chapter for the early Church. Some have even suggested that the picture of Jesus as the Son of Man and Judge was constructed by the early Church from the imagery of this chapter, and that the Son of Man passages in the Gospels which associate Jesus with the angelic judgement were not a part of Jesus's message. This vision of judgement is also set in the temple, with the great throne and the books of judgement, and a figure like a son of man going up to the throne to be given dominion and power for the great judgement. This chapter has been linked to Psalm 2, where the king goes up to receive his power on the holy mountain, and this is almost certainly correct. The one 'like a son of man' in Daniel's vision is therefore the ancient king-figure taking part in the great king-making ceremony when the anointed one sat on the throne of the Lord and ruled as God's agent. This association of ascension, enthronement and judgement later appears in the Creed's 'ascended into heaven, sits at the right hand . . . to judge', and also in many of the hymns written for Ascension Day which describe going up with clouds to a heavenly throne and kingship:

> See the Conqueror mounts in triumph,
> See the King in royal state
> Riding on the clouds his chariot
> To his heavenly palace gate . . .

And also:

> The head that once was crowned with thorns
> Is crowned with glory now . . .

We can now add to our pattern of vision, knowledge, judgement, ascent and angelic status several more elements: the royal figure called 'a son of man', the Eden temple setting with the river of life-giving water, the lamp representing both the presence of God and the Tree of Life whose fruits made man immortal (Gen. 3.22), and the clouds which took a son of man figure to heaven.

Before we trace this vision imagery and its associations through into the New Testament, we must look at the form in which the vision is cast. First, it is never the vision of God simply as the climax of a spiritual ascent. Contemplation of the Great Glory is always the preliminary to a commission to act as God's agent. Second, the visions are always described in terms of earthly things. (See the next chapter on parables.) We are always told that they are *like* their earthly counterparts, not that they *are* that thing. This pattern of correspondences is crucial for our appreciation of the apocalyptists' visions; God could be perceived by the human mind and was not unknowable, but he could not be totally described in earthly terms. Language can take us to the point where vision is possible, but earthly things are a part of the vision. Thus Exodus 24.10 describes the pavement under the heavenly throne as if it were of sapphire. Ezekiel 1 describes fire like bronze, the likeness of living creatures . . . like burning coals . . . like torches . . . like lightning. 1 Enoch 14 describes something like a crystal floor, a ceiling like the path of the stars. John sees the throne and one seated on it like jasper and carnelian, like emerald, and in front of the throne something like a sea of glass, like crystal (Rev. 4.3–6). The vision of God was related to experience, though beyond it; earthly things were part of the vision, and action resulted from it.

The Fourth Gospel is full of the imagery derived from this experience of ascent and vision in the temple. There are ascent and descent motifs: 'No one has ascended into heaven but he who descended from heaven, the Son of Man' (John 3.13); 'Then what if you were to see the Son of Man ascending to where he was before?' (6.62); 'Do not hold me, for I have not yet ascended to the Father' (20.17). Frequently the setting is the temple: 'The Passover of the Jews was at hand . . . In the temple he found those who were selling oxen and sheep' (2.13–14); 'Afterward, Jesus found him in the temple' (5.14); 'About the middle of the feast Jesus went into the temple and taught' (7.14); see also 8.2 and 10.23.

Jesus had been in the presence of God, and he speaks of what he has heard and seen there; 'Truly, truly, I say to you, we speak of what we know, and bear witness to what we have seen' (3.11); 'He who comes from above is above all; he who is of the earth belongs to the earth, and of the earth he speaks; he who comes from heaven is above all' (3.31–2); 'it is not I alone that judge, but I and he who sent me' (8.16); 'I declare to the world what I have heard from him' (8.26), also 8.28, 38, 47; 'the Father who sent me has himself given me commandment what to say and what to speak' (12.49).

Jesus is a royal figure, a son of God: 'Rabbi, you are the Son of God! You are the King of Israel!' (1.49); 'we have believed, and have come to know, that you are the Holy One of God' (6.69); 'my kingship is not from this world' (18.36). He uses the temple imagery of water (7.37) and light (8.12). Like the ancient Messiahs he is the earthly representative of God: 'My Father is working still, and I am working' (5.17). He is honoured with his name: 'that all may honour the Son, even as they honour the Father' (5.23); 'If any one serves me . . . the Father will honour him' (12.26); 'Holy Father, keep them in thy name, which thou hast given me' (17.11). His will is the will of God: 'For I have come down from heaven, not to do my own will, but the will of him who sent me' (6.38). He is the earthly manifestation of the glory of God: 'Jesus . . . manifested his glory' (2.11); 'How can you believe, who receive glory from one another and do not seek the glory that comes from the only God?' (5.44).

Those who see Jesus achieve what others had achieved only by the vision of the throne, the vision of God: they are transformed by the experience and become angelic. They live the life of heaven and have passed through death: 'he who sees me sees him who sent me' (12.45); 'He who has seen me has seen the Father' (14.9). What the apocalyptists would have called knowledge and the status of an angel, the Fourth Gospel calls eternal life: 'For this is the will of my Father, that every one who sees the Son and believes in him should have eternal life' (6.40; cf. I John 3.2); compare also 5.24 and 8.51. What but a sharp criticism can lie behind John 5.37, which says that the Jews have neither seen nor heard God? They think that eternal life is to be found in their Scriptures. Only those sent by God have seen him (6.46); only the son has made him known (1.18). Jesus has the role of the Son of Man, the Judge: 'the Father . . . has given him authority to execute judgment, because he is the Son of man' (5.26–27); cf. 8.15–16.

The clearest points of contact with the royal mythology of the angel world are in the recurring theme of the 'lifting up' of the Son of Man. Since lifting up referred to the ascent of the royal figure to receive his angel status, we see the bitter irony of John 19.7. It was the angels, those who did not die, who were called sons of God, yet here according to 'a law' the Son of God has to be lifted up and then die. The man (in the code of the apocalyptists a *man* meant an angel figure, and, as we shall see, in Jewish interpretation of Scripture 'man' was often thought to be a secret designation for the Messiah) is finally dressed as a king (19.5) and taken away to his lifting up. The writer of the Fourth Gospel was a master of irony, but many of his points cannot be appreciated if divorced from the Enochic frame of reference.

Apart from the Fourth Gospel, we find a significant pattern in the Beatitudes; Jesus speaks of those who will have the kingdom of heaven, those who will be sons of God, and those who will see God (Matthew 5.3–12). Paul also knew this experience of ascent to heaven (2 Cor. 12.1–4), but his great chapter on love (1 Cor. 13) seems to be a criticism of those who placed too much emphasis upon it; the tongues of angels, prophetic gifts, knowledge of mysteries and power to work miracles are all as nothing in comparison with love. And now we see only dimly; the vision face to face is yet to be. With this reserve, Paul is only being true to his Jewish background. He had been brought up with a zeal for the Law, and the Law stood for the descendants of the Deuteronomists, those whom we suspect to have outlawed the visionaries in the first place. Two centuries earlier, Ecclesiasticus had warned against the quest for heavenly knowledge:

> Seek not what is too difficult for you,
> nor investigate what is beyond your power.
> Reflect upon what has been assigned to you,
> for you do not need what is hidden.
> Do not meddle with what is beyond your tasks,

for matters too great for human understanding have been
shown you.
For their hasty judgement has led many astray,
and wrong opinion has caused their thoughts to slip.

(Ecclus 3.18–25)

2 Esdras, written at the end of the first century AD, said that ascent was
not possible: 'I never went down into the deep or as yet into hell,
neither did I ever ascend into heaven' (2 Esd. 4.8). A second-century
rabbi used Psalm 115.16 – 'The heavens are the Lord's heavens, but
the earth he has given to the sons of men' – to argue that ascent was not
possible. No one had gone up to heaven, neither had the glory of God
ever come to earth. This might have been directed against the Jewish
mystics, or even against Christian claims.

In the early Christian centuries there was a great deal of Jewish
speculation about the throne of God, and whether or not it was
possible for human beings to experience ascent. The divine throne as
described by Ezekiel was a chariot (in Hebrew, *merkabah*), and these
experiences became known as Merkabah mysticism. There are several
of the mystical texts; some tell of one heaven, others of seven. Paul
knew several heavens, for he claims to have ascended to the third
(2 Cor. 12.2). These ascent experiences described the throne, the
angels, the fires and the sensations of both heat and cold; they were
considered very dangerous. There is a famous story, told in several
versions, of four rabbis who entered Paradise. Only one, the great
Rabbi Akiba, ascended and descended safely. The others, we are told,
'looked' and did not survive the experience. Those who cultivated
these experiences were called the 'descenders into the chariot', an odd
name for those who ascended, but one which tells us that these ancient
mystics were more sophisticated than we often suppose. It was only
forty years ago that the American theologian Paul Tillich suggested
(as though it were something new) that depth language was more
appropriate for God than height language. When these ideas were
popularized fifteen years later in John Robinson's famous book
Honest to God, a great storm of protest greeted the suggestion that God
'up there' was no longer an appropriate way of thinking and speaking.
Yet the ancient wise men, with their descending ascents and their
parables linking earth and heaven, had been saying this long ago. Our
over-literal minds have been preoccupied with the picture, and we
have missed the other side of the parable. Jesus himself said, 'the

kingdom of God is within you' (Luke 17.21); perhaps he meant the same thing. There is a longer version of this saying in the Gospel of Thomas which makes the meaning clearer: 'The Kingdom is inside of you, and it is outside of you. When you come to know yourselves, then you will become known, and you will realize that it is you who are the sons of the living Father' (Thomas 3.1–2).

Christians continued to use the chariot and ascent imagery. There is a collection of early Christian hymns known as the Odes of Solomon. Whether they were originally Christian or Jewish is debated, but they certainly became Christian. A few of them were first rediscovered about two hundred years ago in a Coptic version, and since then almost complete versions in Syriac have been found, and one Ode in Greek. Ode 38 is very similar to the account of Enoch's ascent and travels:

> I went up into the light of truth as into a chariot
> And the Truth led me and caused me to come
> And caused me to pass over chasms and cliffs
> And saved me from cliffs and valleys . . .
> And there was no danger for me, because I constantly
> walked with Him.

Eusebius the church historian tells the less happy tale (*Histories* 5.16.17) of one Theodotus, who ascended to heaven in ecstacy but perished miserably as a result. The most detailed description of an ascent is in the account of the martyrdom of St Perpetua, who died in Carthage in AD 202. St Perpetua was granted three visions before her death. In the first she saw a ladder, set with terrible weapons, which she had to climb. At the top was a beautiful garden where there was a shepherd dressed in white who welcomed her. A fellow martyr, St Satyrus, also had a vision in which he ascended after his death to an angelic garden in which was a building with walls of light. Guardian angels dressed in white put white robes on all who entered, and inside he heard the angels singing 'Holy, Holy, Holy', just as Isaiah and Enoch had done. The description of the throne, the white robes and the angel song could well be a memory of Revelation; the walls of light could have come from Enoch's description; and the dangers of the heavenly ladder are the common experience of mystics. The garden, however, takes us right back to the ancient kings, and their ascent to the presence of God in the heavenly Garden of Eden, the heavenly temple.

The vision of God remained important in the early Church. We see this in the histories, in the teaching and also in the worship. St Irenaeus was the bishop of Lyons in southern France at the end of the second century. He had come from Asia Minor, from Smyrna near Ephesus, where he had known the martyr Polycarp, who in turn, claimed Irenaeus, had known the apostle John when he had worked in Ephesus in his later years. It therefore comes as no surprise that in the writings of Irenaeus, who was the most important theologian of the period, we find developed the ideas of the vision of God which are hinted at in the Fourth Gospel. Perhaps Irenaeus was explaining them in more detail because he was writing a book, *Against Heresies*. God, he said, had become human in Jesus and brought the vision of God to all humankind. The vision of God gave eternal life; it made human beings into sons of God. It made them divine. This vision of God also gave knowledge, although by this time knowledge meant the heavenly secrets revealed by Jesus to his followers. Irenaeus does not emphasize the sacrificial or conquest imagery of Christ's death. He truly died as proof that he was truly human. Some people at the time were saying that he was not really human, but only appeared so. Irenaeus's great emphasis was upon the union of divine and human in Jesus, the incarnation, the possibility of God in human terms. He saw a whole life, and not just a death, as the means whereby human beings had been restored to their status as sons of God. (This idea has its deepest roots in the parable teaching of the wise men of Israel; see chapter 5.) It was the union of heaven and earth in Jesus which made the vision possible, and its benefits available to all.

This pattern of ideas became very important in the later mystical traditions of the Eastern Churches, in which the vision of the divine light was said to transform and deify the soul. This light was the same light as had been manifested in the great visions of the Old Testament, when God had revealed his glory, and it was the light which the apostles had seen at the transfiguration. The light was always there; the moments of vision, such as the transfiguration, were moments when the disciples were transformed and made able to see what was really there. Francis Thompson's poem 'No Strange Land' expresses this well:

> The angels keep their ancient places; –
> Turn but a stone and start a wing!
> 'Tis ye, 'tis your estranged faces,
> That miss the many splendoured thing.

This is not so very different from some of the sayings of Jesus in the Gospel of Thomas. 'Split a piece of wood, and I am there. Lift up the stone, and you will find Me there . . . [The] Kingdom of the Father is spread out upon the earth, and men do not see it' (Thomas 77.2; 113.2).

There is another area where the heavenly vision is still remembered, perhaps more accessible to most of us than the mysticism of either the Eastern Church or the ancient writings preserved by gnostic Christians in Egypt. In the great visions which form the Similitudes, Enoch hears the song of the angels before the throne of God (1 Enoch 39). It is the same as Isaiah heard in his vision, 'Holy, holy, holy is the Lord of hosts [spirits]'. John hears it in his vision (Rev. 4.8), and it is used in the eucharistic prayers at the point where we remind ourselves that our worship joins that of heaven:

> Therefore with Angels and Archangels,
> and with all the company of heaven,
> we laud and magnify thy glorious Name;
> evermore praising thee, and saying,
> Holy, holy, holy, Lord God of hosts,
> heaven and earth are full of thy glory:
> Glory be to thee, O Lord most High.

In the Orthodox Church priests pray that angels may minister with them at the Eucharist, and in the old Roman eucharistic prayer there is the request that God's holy angel will take the bread and wine to the heavenly altar. Christian worship continues the vision of God; this is why the Eastern Churches have their great domes to represent the heavens, with Christ the Judge at the centre, and the worshippers below, surrounded by pictures of the saints with whom they are joined. It is said that this vision of heaven was so powerful that it even led to the conversion of Russia. Vladimir the pagan ruler of Kiev sent ambassadors to Constantinople, where they saw the great liturgy of the Church and knew that that was where God dwelt with men. When Vladimir was converted in 988, he brought this vision of God to Russia, along with Christian teachers and Christian books. Among them was a book of Enoch – not the one we know from the Ethiopic text, but another related text which has survived only in Old Slavonic, the language of the Russian Church. It is known as 2 Enoch, or the Secrets of Enoch, and is another account of great visions of God and the heavenly world. Ancient manuscripts of the book are now treasured in such places as Leningrad, Moscow and Belgrade, and the angels of 2 Enoch sing the same song as did the angels of Isaiah and Enoch (2 Enoch 21).

In all this we have travelled a long way from Enoch's vision of the great throne, which threw such a startling new light on to the religion of the third century BC and gave us a glimpse into the world of the ancient temple. But even at the furthest points of the journey there was the same vision and the same insight, proof of how fundamental was this experience, and how far-reaching was its influence. It has been expressed in hymns from the very earliest times, and is still the subject of modern ones. The Orthodox Church's ancient Liturgy of St James, which we know as

Let all mortal flesh keep silence, and with fear and trembling stand;
Ponder nothing earthly-minded, for with blessing in his hand,
Christ our God to earth descendeth, our full homage to demand,

and the increasingly popular modern hymn

Majesty, worship his Majesty
Unto Jesus be glory, honour and praise.
Majesty, kingdom authority, flows from his throne
Unto His own, His anthem raise,

are both derived from the same root. And between them have come

Come, let us join our cheerful songs
With Angels round the throne,

whose author was born in the seventeenth century;

Holy, Holy, Holy! Lord God Almighty!
Early in the morning our song shall rise to thee,

whose author was born in the eighteenth century; and

My God, how wonderful thou art,
Thy majesty how bright,
How beautiful thy mercy-seat,
In depths of burning light,

whose author was born in the nineteenth century. All these hymns use the imagery we have traced to Enoch and the Enochic tradition: the divine status of the king who was the earthly representative of God (we shall explore this in chapter 7); the water imagery flowing from the great throne in the ancient Garden of Eden; the angelic song around the throne; and the association of the heavenly throne of God not only with indescribable brightness, as in the mystics' visions, but also with the mercy seat, which was in the actual earthly temple.

When we begin to unpack the lost tradition, we realize that it has never really been lost. It has passed into familiar language and has thus been overlooked. The recovery of Enoch prompts us to look more closely at what is all around us, lest we too miss 'the many splendoured thing'.

Chapter 5

The Parables

The second section of Enoch is called the Similitudes or Parables, but it does not contain parables in the sense that we normally use that word. 'Parable' usually conjures up for us the stories that Jesus told about the mustard seed, the measure of yeast or the good shepherd. Enoch's parables are not like that; they are visions. The section begins with Enoch describing the vision of wisdom which he saw, and the words of the Holy One which he had to speak. He says he received three parables for those who live on earth. We must therefore look for a meaning of the word 'parable' broad enough to cover Enoch's type of parable, the gospel parables, and several other examples of parables in the Old Testament.

Unfortunately, the words for parable in Hebrew (*mashal*) and Greek (*parabole*) are not always translated into English by the word parable, and therefore are not obvious in the English versions. This should be a warning to us. If the English word parable with its usual meanings was felt to be an inappropriate word in most cases, then on occasions when it is used it is probably inappropriate too. We have to imagine a whole set of ideas which the Hebrew mind could put under one heading, but which to us do not seem to belong together. The problem of finding one English word to be the equivalent to *mashal* is a clear example of how different our thought-world is from that of New Testament times. If Jesus taught in parables, how well have we understood that teaching? In Numbers 23.7,18 and Job 27.1 the word translated by 'discourse'; in Isaiah 14.4 and Micah 2.4 by 'taunt song'; in Ezekiel 17.2; 20.49; 24.3 by 'allegory'; in 1 Samuel 10.12 by 'proverb' – indeed the whole book of Proverbs is the book of Parables and Solomon spoke three thousand parables (1 Kings 4.32), a sign that he was a wise man. In the New Testament, apart from in the Gospels, the word is used in Hebrews 9.9, 'symbolic', and Hebrews 11.19, 'figuratively'.

There have been many complex arguments about the meaning of *mashal*, and it would be impossible to summarize all of them briefly. Two things, however, are clear: the parable/proverb was associated

65

with the wise men and their wisdom, and it worked, like Hebrew poetry, on the principle of parallels, comparing one thing with another. Perhaps we can begin by saying that the wise men saw an overall pattern in all God's world, whether visible or invisible, and used the correspondences to teach. There were others in the ancient world whom we call by other names, usually magicians, who also worked with this knowledge of parallels. They believed that a knowledge of the correspondences in creation enabled distortions to be corrected and put right. This was the basis of their magic and their healings. It should not surprise us to discover that Jesus, the speaker of parables and the healer, was described and remembered by many in the ancient world as a magician. This is not so slanderous a title as it might seem to us with our modern ideas of what a magician is.

The 'parable' which is a short pithy saying (what we should call a proverb), often gives us both sides of the comparison. The biblical book of Proverbs is almost entirely this type of parable. The longer story/parable gives only one side of the parallelism, and leaves the reader to work out what is really being said. When Jesus gave the parable, 'the kingdom of heaven . . . is like a grain of mustard seed' (Mark 4.30–32), we know that he was actually talking about the growth of the Kingdom, the power, of God. He used the earthly to teach about the heavenly. On the other hand, when Isaiah gave the parable about the proud star climbing above the throne of God Most High, we know he was actually talking about the downfall of the king of Babylon. He used the heavenly to teach about the earthly. The parables (English: 'discourses') in Numbers 23–4 are reports of the visions of Balaam, one who 'hears the words of God, and knows the knowledge of the Most High, who sees the vision of the Almighty' (Num. 24.16). The parables (English: 'allegories') of Ezekiel are from someone who had visions of the throne chariot of God (Ezek. 1;10), and who was lifted by the hair and carried by the Spirit of Jerusalem (Ezek. 8.3). Even Solomon, to whom are attributed the less exotic parables of the book of Proverbs, had a dream in which God appeared to him. Solomon asked for the gift of wisdom, in order to rule God's people (1 Kings 3.5–14). Teaching in parables was a characteristic of wise men, as we have often been told. But the wise men were also visionaries, and this aspect is less emphasized. The Book of Proverbs does not seem to be the work of a visionary, yet the two biblical wise men of whom we know anything, Daniel and Joseph, were both dreamers.

Many of the parables, the sayings of the wise men, give the heavenly side of the parallel, in order that the hearer may work out the earthly application. Because of the very nature of the 'heavenly' aspect of the parable, it was given in the form of a vision, in Enoch's case called a 'vision of wisdom'. It was an insight into the secrets of the creation, as that creation was experienced in an earthly, material existence. It was a revelation, an apocalypse. That is what apocalypse means. Often the visions dealt with the great judgement, whether of Israel or of her enemies, but always there was an earthly correspondence to what was seen. The prophets were associated especially with this type of vision, even though their oracles were not always called parables. The prophets believed that they had been especially privileged to stand in the presence of God, and to know the reality behind their earthly experience. They could then report what they had 'seen' (the prophets 'saw' the word of the Lord, e.g. Isa. 1.1; Amos 1.1; Obad. 1; Mic. 1.1; Nahum 1.1). This is what was meant by the prophets being able to foretell the future; they could see what was going to happen, because they had seen its heavenly counterpart, and knew the divine plan. Thus their words were feared. Much has been written about the difference between prophecy and 'wisdom'. For a long time we have been required to label writings as one or the other. This is a false distinction, caused by our way of making definitions.

The three parables of Enoch each describe the great judgement on the kings and the mighty; it is clear from the punishments that these are the fallen angels, even though they are also the kings. Here we see the basic myth of the angels again, forming the framework of Enoch's parable, the insight being that the evil kings would meet their judgement. It is here that we first become aware of one of the characteristics of the parable. The judgement described is not something that happens in another state of life, nor does it necessarily happen in the future. It can be a description of present reality, the unseen being the counterpart of what is actually happening. Nor do we have to think of a parable or vision as having only one specific meaning or application. We tend to think that story parables are relevant again and again, but that visions have a particular message for a particular situation. This is not so. Visions too were relevant to more than one situation. When we look at the more familiar parables of the Gospels, where the Kingdom of heaven is described as a measure of yeast growing, or a pearl to be found, we do not think that this insight applies to only one particular occasion, to one particular pearl or measure of yeast. It is a general observation. So too with the visions. They were relevant to particular circumstances, but were also of abiding value. That is why the words of the prophets were recorded and kept. It is therefore wrong to talk about prophecies being re-used by later generations, as though that were something unnatural or second rate. The insight of the vision was an insight into an unchanging reality. All prophecy had a meaning waiting to be found. The written form of the prophecy became itself like a *mashal*, a parable. The text itself gave only one side of the parallel, and the wise interpretation had to give the other. We see this process in the biblical commentaries written by the Qumran community. They treated prophetic writings as mysteries needing interpretation, just as others treated visions. Prophecy was not a thing of the remote past. It was a window into the eternal present.

We often think of 'the prophets' as a particular group of people who spoke in the distant past, and then somehow ceased to exist. 'The Prophets' became the name for a group of writings. But prophecy did not cease to exist or to be written, even though there were some who sought to curb and discredit it, perhaps in the interests of stability or uniformity (e.g. Zech. 13.2–6). Prophecy could not and cannot be controlled, and is by its very nature disturbing. It takes as its point of reference something other than the status quo. The Deuteronomists never sorted out what they thought about prophecy, because they were first and foremost organizers and lawyers; prophecy was a problem to them. At one stage they demanded proof that a prophet's words had been fulfilled (Deut. 18.21–22). Since these fulfilments usually happened after the death of the prophet, the true prophets were the dead ones. But when even proof became dangerous (Deut. 13.1–5), only orthodoxy, agreeing with Moses, was acceptable as true prophecy. A great number of people did not accept this, and continued to believe in living prophecy outside the constraint of the Law. The Enochic tradition is a good example of this. By New Testament times some books were prophetic interpretations of earlier works, others were completely new compositions. Prophecy was important in the early Church. John the Baptist and Jesus were spoken of as prophets. We read of Agabus in Acts 11.27–30, and of prophecy being a recognized ministry (1 Cor. 12.29). Throughout the New Testament we read of prophecies being fulfilled. This ability to relate prophecy to current events was in itself an aspect of prophecy, establishing the pattern of correspondences.

The vision parables of Enoch were not a new form of parable, nor was the content of the visions anything new. For centuries the prophets of Israel had seen the inevitable judgement upon evil which was a part of the natural order. There is a picture of this judgement of the kings and the mighty as early as Isaiah 24.21, where the Lord punishes the host of heaven in the heavens, and the kings of the earth on the earth. The two are in parallel; in some way they are each other. This is exactly like the picture in Psalm 89, where the roles and powers of God in the heavens are exactly mirrored in the roles and powers of his anointed king on earth. The king was the earthly manifestation of the power of God. It is this type of thinking which lies behind so many of the mysterious verses of the Fourth Gospel, e.g. John 5.30: 'I can do nothing on my own authority; as I hear, I judge; and my judgment is just, because I seek not my own will but the will of him who sent me'; or John 10.25: 'The works that I do in my Father's name, they bear witness to me'; or John 10.30: 'I and the Father are one [thing].' In Enoch we find the same quite explicit parallelisms. 1 Enoch 43.4 says that the stars in heaven are the saints on earth who believe in the name of the Lord of Spirits (this is Enoch's version of the title Lord of Hosts). Compare here Daniel 12.3, where the righteous will shine for ever like the stars, and also Job 38.33, where the Lord asks Job: 'Do you know the ordinances of the heavens? Can you establish their rule on the earth?' Or even the Lord's Prayer: 'Thy will be done, on earth as it is in heaven' (Matt. 6.10). 1 Enoch 71.14 says that the Son of Man, presumably a heavenly figure, is Enoch. In other words, Enoch on earth is to have the role of the heavenly Son of Man and bring the message of judgement to the fallen ones. In the Fourth Gospel this earthly role of the Son of Man is given to Jesus (John 5.27). He was to announce the judgement.

We must therefore assume that the whole picture given in Enoch's parables is the heavenly parallel to an earthly reality. There are three parables, each saying more or less the same things. The details differ, but this is probably a sign that we have three ancient versions of the traditions side by side. The first vision describes the great upheaval when the congregation of the righteous appears. The kings and the mighty perish before the throne of God, and Enoch is transported to see the dwellings of the righteous. He sees the secrets of the heavens, and how the kingdoms are divided and the actions of men are weighed. Compare here the message of the wise man Daniel to King Belshazzar (Dan. 5.26–28): 'God has numbered the days of your kingdom . . . you have been weighed . . . your kingdom is divided'. The words are very similar, showing that the patterns and concerns of the wise men were not arbitrary, but were very deeply rooted in the traditions of Israel.

In the second parable the Elect One sits on the throne of glory to begin the great judgement. Heaven and earth are transformed, and Enoch sees a vision of the Son of Man and the 'Head of Days', not unlike that in Dan 7.13. The books are opened and the name of the Son of Man is revealed. This Elect One is given the spirit of wisdom. (Son of Man and Elect One are titles for the same figure, but from the different traditions.) We are then told that the mountains become powerless before the face of the Lord of Spirits, a curious picture until we realize that the mountains were believed to contain heavenly powers, some of whom were evil. In 1 Enoch 18.13 Enoch sees the fallen angels like great burning mountains; Jeremiah 51.25 describes Babylon as a destroying mountain which was to be burnt, and a burning mountain falls from heaven in John's vision (Rev. 8.8). Again, we have an indication that the imagery and concerns of Enoch were those of the prophets and the old religion of Israel, which were later taken up and used by the early Church. In this second great vision Enoch sees the judgement on Asael, presided over by the Elect One, another version of the tale in the Book of the Watchers.

In the third vision Enoch sees more heavenly secrets, and learns the duties of various angels before witnessing the judgement of the kings and the mighty by the Elect One. In this vision the throne is surrounded by the angels and by the righteous, presumably those who have been transformed into their angelic state (cf. 1 Cor. 6.2–3: 'Do you not know that the saints will judge the world? . . . that we are to judge angels?'). Enoch sees the punishment of the angels and learns their names. Twenty-one names are given, most of which end in –el, the word meaning God. The angels had godlike powers. But these names are not the same as the angel names in the Book of the Watchers, and this is important, because the names of the angels were vital in the business of healing and exorcism. If one knew the name of the evil one, it could be bound and commanded (cf. Mark 5.9, where Jesus asks the name of the demon, and then drives it out). We know from the historian Josephus that the Essenes had a solemn oath to preserve the names of the angels. They recognized their value and would not lightly have altered them. This shows us that the lists in the Similitudes and the Book of the Watchers could be from different traditions within the Enochic theology. We have no real proof of the age of either, beyond their own claims to be more pure than the ways of the second temple, and therefore presumably more ancient. If they are more ancient, the question arises: 'Why do we hear so little of angels in the Old Testament? What happened to them?' The vision ends with the revelation of the great oath (see chapter 6), and there follows the short but cryptic account in which Enoch is designated the Son of Man.

A topic often raised in connection with writings like these is that of dualism, by which can be meant any one, or indeed all, of a number of things. It can be a view of the world which sees the material and the spiritual as entirely different and separate, created by different gods and hostile to each other. The spiritual has to be set free from the material. Or it can mean the struggle between two forces (good and evil variously represented by spirits and angels) for the control of this world or for the control of an individual's life. Or it can be a dualism of time: this world and then the world to come. The dualism which depicts the struggle between good and evil certainly had a place in some Jewish and early Christian writings, but not in Enoch and those directly related to it. The imagery of Enoch is not of a final battle against evil, although there is a struggle in the preceding years. It is of a great trial, the last judgement, where the outcome is never in doubt. The other dualisms which separate spiritual and material and temporal and eternal are not a feature of Enoch, even though this has been suggested. What we see in Enoch is a completely integrated world-view, where heaven and earth are counterparts of each other in one reality, and where time and eternity show the same patterns. The heavenly/spiritual operates through the material world, for good and for evil, and time is the state from which we glimpse eternity. Wise men knew these correspondences and called them parables. If Enoch had been based on a dualism which separated material and spiritual, temporal and eternal, the parables would not have been possible. Our problem is to understand what they were really saying, given that our Western minds think very differently. What they were saying will have been very similar in form to what the New Testament writers were saying, and what the early Christians continued to say. In the Odes of Solomon 34 we read:

> The likeness of that which is below
> Is that which is above;

For everything is from above
And from below there is nothing.

How then is it possible for a vision of the heavenly throne of judgement to be paralleled in the everyday world? How is a glimpse of eternity to be related to life as we live it? Had these visions not been relevant to everyday life and the source of an ongoing theology they would not have survived. The myth of the fallen angels was, as we have seen, applied to several contemporary situations. It had an ongoing relevance, as a pattern for life. Thus it differed from simple predictions of the future, which when fulfilled were no longer relevant and needed. The judgement described in Enoch's parables took place again and again. The prophets had used the imagery for Babylon and Tyre, and Daniel had used it for the Seleucid kings, yet it was still thought to be available for application to another set of circumstances. We have to see the parables of Enoch in the same way; the heavenly vision of the judgement states a general truth about the nature of reality. This is how we must read the central section of Revelation (Rev. 4–18). The great events in heaven have effects on earth, e.g. the four angelic horsemen (Rev. 6.2–8) terrorize the earth even though they are heavenly figures. The business of the judgement is part of the reality of things, the heavenly parallel which lies behind and beyond, and enables us to see the structure of what happens around us. This idea of one pattern story, one parable which serves to teach and make sense of reality on more than one level, is most familiar to us in our re-enactments of the Last Supper, our recalling of the events of Good Friday and Easter. We believe that these were more than earthly events, and therefore have a continuing place in the pattern of things as they really are.

We see the apocalyptists' attitudes to time and eternity in the Book of Dreams, where we read the history of Israel. The period from the fall of Samaria to the writer's time, about five hundred years, is said to be under the rule of seventy shepherds (i.e. seventy angels). The seventy exist simultaneously; they are summoned together before the Lord of the sheep, and receive their orders at the same time. They then act in succession for what the writer calls seventy periods, after which they are all summoned and judged together. The great angel figures who manifest themselves in history and politics are perceived by humankind only in their temporal aspect. They exist 'before' this and 'after' this, but they exist in a dimension outside time, which we, as human beings, cannot comprehend and therefore cannot strictly describe as being 'before' or 'after' anything else. These beings are part of the eternal order which exists in its entirety behind and beyond every manifestation of it which we perceive. We must try to think of 'time' and 'beyond time', which is perhaps a better description than 'eternity', since eternity has come to mean simply an extremely long stretch of time, and this is not what the apocalyptists meant. Time is measured by material things, their relationships and their growth and decay. Beyond the material world there cannot be time as we understand it; but just as we have to describe the heavenly in terms of the earthly, so too we have to describe what is beyond time in terms which derive from our experience of time.

In certain places, and in certain people, the two creations became one. There was a Jewish belief that the patriarch Jacob was a man, but that Israel (which we usually think of as his other name) was his angel counterpart, the name meaning 'a man who sees God'. Enoch the wise man had a place in both worlds. The story of the transfiguration of Jesus points to exactly this; that Jesus was at the intersection of the two worlds, and the chosen few were able to see through to the other reality. It is the idea of an existence outside time which gives us the New Testament pictures of Jesus existing before he was actually born – 'the Word became flesh' (John 1.14); 'the first-born of all creation' (Col. 1.15); 'a Son . . . through whom also he created the world' (Heb. 1.2), etc. – and living on after his physical death. He belonged to the existence outside time, as well as to this world. He even took the name of the great angels; he was described as a shepherd. The temple too was a place of heaven and earth (cf. Ps. 11.4: 'The Lord is in his holy temple, the Lord's throne is in heaven'). The anointed kings were people who bridged the two creations, whence the claim in the Fourth Gospel: 'I and the Father are one [thing]' (John 10.30); 'Do you not believe that I am in the Father and the Father in me?' (John 14.10). Christians were also to bridge the two creations; the Gospel of Thomas attributes this cryptic saying to Jesus: 'When you make the two one, you will become the sons of man, and when you say, "Mountain, move away," it will move away' (Thomas 106). It was this of the two worlds which was the sign and the function of a Son and, when it was achieved, great powers resulted.

If we read Hebrews 9 in this way we find the temple as the place of intersection of the two worlds, and the Melchizedek priest as the person who functions in both worlds. The temple and its rituals were already believed in New Testament times to be the earthly aspect of the heavenly reality, and the Messiah was already believed to be a priest like Melchizedek, a priest for eternity (Ps. 110.4). What seems to us an elaborate argument is quite logical in this way of thinking. Scholars have scrutinized this chapter for subtleties of Greek philosophy, but the clue to understanding it is given in Hebrews 9.9. The temple is a 'parable' for the present age, it is the earthly part of a parallelism whose great reality lies beyond. Some of the fragment texts from Qumran, 'The Songs of the Sabbath Sacrifice', show exactly the same picture; the rituals of the heavenly temple are the counterparts of those on earth.

The Fourth Gospel is also full of this imagery of ascent and descent, above and below, depicting Jesus as the link between the two worlds: 'unless one is born from above, he cannot see the kingdom of God' (John 3.3); 'No one has ascended into heaven but he who descended from heaven, the son of man' (John 3.13); 'He who comes from above is above all; he who is of the earth belongs to the earth, and of the earth he speaks; he who comes from heaven is above all' (John 3.31. cf. also 6.33, 38, 62; 8.14, etc.).

Thus too we must read the seer John and the great vision of Revelation. He was able to see beyond the present reality to the pattern which lay behind it and determined it. Revelation 4.1 says: 'I will show you what must take place after this'. 'After this' can also be translated 'beyond this', and the phrase almost certainly has both meanings here. John was seeing into the future only in so far as he was being placed at the beginning of a very familiar pattern. Most of the bizarre imagery of the book can be found in other apocalyptic writings. He was able to see how it would all work out in his situation. The seer was able to understand both present and future because he had a pattern. This pattern of Revelation is still relevant, not because it was a prediction that did not happen and is therefore somehow still 'live' and looking for fulfilment, but because it is an insight into the eternal pattern and will go on being a framework within which we can attempt to set the problem of evil and its end.

All this is very complicated and foreign to our ways of thinking. If we allow ourselves to think in terms of dualism, time separate from eternity, material separate from spiritual, we drive a wedge through the very heart of the original gospel insight. We find ourselves with the idea of an 'eternal' life which starts only after physical death; with an idea that bodily needs and pleasures are unspiritual and to be shunned (what terrible consequences this has had for women, who by their very nature represent bodily needs and pleasures to the all-male body who developed Christian theology!); with the idea that the Kingdom of God is something remote and unworldly, a place of harps and white robes, the opiate of the people. If we force ourselves back to the integrated world-view of the apocalyptists and the first Christians, we find that eternal life is earthly life already linked to and intersected with, the other dimension, allowing what is beyond to suffuse and transform what is here. This is the essential meaning of the Eucharist. We find that the human body is the vehicle and channel of the Spirit of God, the means by which we give and receive love, and exercise our functions as incarnate sons of God, renewing the creation. The New Testament tells us that the body is the temple, and the temple was the place between heaven and earth where God was present. Our bodies are the bridge between the two creations.

We also find that the Kingdom of God is something here and now, God's power breaking through in this world. We recover the vision of the older Messiahs, the kings of Jerusalem, who were believed to be the link between heaven and earth. They sat on the throne of God (1 Chron. 29.23), and their kingdom, though derived from the realm of the angels, was a very earthly reality. Psalm 72 shows how these ancient sons of God brought the Kingdom of heaven to earth; they brought justice, righteousness, deliverance and redemption; even the earth responded with fertility and prosperity. Jesus described the Kingdom of God as growing (Mark 4), or being discovered like a great treasure (Matt. 13.44), but above all it was 'among you' or 'within you' (Luke 17.21). Scholars have long debated whether the Kingdom is present or future, or something in tension in between. Looked at through the eyes of the apocalyptists, these are not relevant questions.

Enoch's parables, the pictures of heaven which show us the truth about the earth, are described not only as parables but also as a vision of wisdom. They were an insight into the true nature of the world, life, creation. They showed the essential coherence of all things in one great pattern; as above, so below. In Francis Thompson's words again:

> O World invisible, we view thee,
> O world intangible, we touch thee,
> O world unknowable, we know thee,
> Inapprehensible we clutch thee!

Enoch does not need to raise the question of later thinkers: 'How can the human mind know anything about God, when its only experience is of this world?' Enoch knows only one all-encompassing world, and this knowledge was wisdom.

But what else do we know about wisdom? The wise were exalted to the stars, to live the angelic life. Enoch was not in the tradition of the fallen Adam, where such wisdom was forbidden because it opened man's eyes and made him like God (or godlike). The story in Genesis says, in effect, that Adam was condemned to remain blind, and never to achieve his godlike state. The God depicted in Genesis seems to be frightened, or jealous, of man in his godlike state. Mortality is the only way to keep him in check. The Enoch tradition experienced God differently, and had no fear of the angelic life of the wise ones. The early Christian tradition grew from this, with its belief in a life that is more than mortal, and in the acquired status of sons of God. Its sacramental theology affirmed that the divine could transform and recreate the material world. It is curious that in Christian practice the angelic life became one of denying the world rather than of transforming it, even though the Greek Fathers retained the idea that God became man so that man could become divine.

Chapter 6

The Cosmic Covenant

At two places in the Similitudes we read of a great oath which binds the forces of the creation. At first sight this seems to be an idea which is so primitive, so bizarre, that it cannot have any more relevance to twentieth-century Christianity than, say, the exact dimensions of Noah's ark. When the idea of the cosmic covenant is explored, however, it proves to be one of the most significant aspects of Enochic theology, and one which comes very near to much of what our environmentalists are saying today. It provides a totally new way of looking at the creation. I say 'totally new' because, even though I Enoch was known and used by the first Christians, this aspect of its theology was lost along with so much else. As a result, there are several parts of the New Testament which we no longer understand in their original way.

In the first vision Enoch sees how all the heavenly bodies are kept on their courses in accordance with the oath which binds them (I Enoch 41), and in the third vision he sees the workings of the great oath (I Enoch 69). The first part of this text is confused, but we are told that the powerful oath was entrusted to the archangel Michael. The oath secures the order of the creation, holds the heavens firm and the earth secure. It keeps the sea in check with a barrier of sand. It orders the deeps and regulates the course of the sun and moon. Then there is a list of all the other forces of creation: spirits of water, winds, thunders, hail, frost, mist, rain and dew. They all function safely through the strength of the great oath, and they praise the Lord of Spirits. The text here seems to be in the form of a poem or hymn, with a refrain at the end of each section:

And they are strong through his oath:
And the heaven was suspended before the world was created,
And for ever.

And through it the earth was founded upon the water,
And from the secret recesses of the mountains come beautiful waters,
From the creation of the world and unto eternity.

And through that oath the sea was created,
And as its foundation He set for it the sand against the time of (its)
    anger,
And it dare not pass beyond it from the creation of the world unto
    eternity.
And through that oath are the depths made fast,
And abide and stir not from their place from eternity to eternity.
And through that oath the sun and moon complete their course,
And deviate not from their ordinance from eternity to eternity.

And through that oath the stars complete their course,
And He calls them by their names,
And they answer Him from eternity to eternity . . .
And this oath is mighty over them,
And through it [they are preserved and] their paths are preserved,
And their course is not destroyed. (1 Enoch 69.16–21, 25)

The Benedicite, the Song of the Three Children in the Apocrypha, has
a very similar theme: all creation praises and acknowledges its
Creator. It looks as though there was once far more of the hymn in
Enoch than presently survives in the third Similitude; it breaks off
rather suddenly.

The idea of creating by binding the forces of creation is very
ancient, more ancient than the account of the creation we read in
Genesis. It is clearly linked to the world of magic, and one which was
widely known among ancient peoples. They believed in a cosmic or
eternal covenant which kept all things in harmony, in accordance with
the divine plan. To break this covenant was to release forces which
could destroy the creation. It is interesting that the Hebrew word for
covenant, *b*ᵉ*rīth*, is thought to be related to the word for binding.
Some say that this was the binding of an agreement between two
parties, in the manner of the covenant at Sinai. But there could be this
other meaning; the binding of the destructive forces. The word for
covenant in Hebrew is also very similar to the word 'create'. Covenant
. . . bind . . . create makes an interesting sequence in the light of the
Enochic picture of creation. Whether or not they are linked we shall
probably never know.

Closely linked to this oath is the 'name' or the 'secret name', which
was the means of enforcing and maintaining the covenant/oath. The
name had been named before the creation, presumably to make the
creation possible.

And at that hour that Son of Man was named
In the presence of the Lord of Spirits,
And his name before the Head of Days.

Yea, before the sun and the signs were created,
Before the stars of the heaven were made,
His name was named before the Lord of Spirits.   (1 Enoch 48.2–3)

This has been taken to mean that Jesus existed before the creation, the pre-existent Messiah. I think it more likely that here in 1 Enoch the Son of Man as the heavenly counterpart of earthly figures was part of the created order of things, and that the means of restoring the creation was provided in the original plan which was outside time and therefore not strictly 'before' anything. Knowing this name added force and strength to the oath. The climax of the last vision of judgement in the Similitudes is the revealing of the 'name' of the Son of Man. This may mean a revelation of his identity, especially as the next section goes on to say that the Son of Man is Enoch, but in the context of the binding oath it is more likely to mean the revelation of an especially powerful name with which to bind the oath, and thus restore the creation to its original state, as it had been before the incursion of evil. The vision ends with the Son of Man passing judgement on all those who had corrupted the earth, binding them so that evil passes away.

Covenant is a very important word in the Bible; the very names by which the two parts are known, Old Testament and New Testament, actually mean Old Covenant and New Covenant. By exploring the ancient concept of the eternal covenant, which is mentioned in the Old Testament but seldom noticed today, we may add another dimension to our understanding of Christianity as the New Covenant.

In the Old Testament a covenant can mean no more than an agreement between two people (e.g. Gen. 31.44, where Jacob and Laban make an agreement). But usually we think of covenant in terms of the covenants made with the great figures of the Old Testament – with Noah, Abraham, David and Moses. Each covenant marks a step forward in the religious history of Israel. After the great flood, God makes a covenant with all living creatures that the earth will never again be destroyed by flood (Gen. 9.8–11). Noah and his family were obliged in their turn never to shed blood, nor to consume it. With Abraham there were two occasions of covenant: the land of Canaan was to be given to his descendants (Gen. 15.18–21), and all his male children had to be circumcised (Gen. 17.9–14). A covenant was made with Moses and the Israelite people at Sinai, when the Ten Commandments were given (Exod. 24.8), and the blood of sacrificial oxen was sprinkled on the altar and on the people to seal the covenant. The royal covenant was made with David (2 Sam. 7), promising to establish his dynasty for ever.

The order in which the covenants are described in the Old Testament is not necessarily the order in which Israel actually became aware of them. The earliest history stories in the Old Testament (e.g. those about Abraham) were not written down at the time when they happened, but were drawn from people's memories and traditions at a much later period. They were used by theologians to illustrate their account of the growth of Israel as a nation, and its increasing awareness of the nature and purposes of God. The covenant with Abraham promising possession of the land of Canaan and numerous descendants was probably woven into that ancient story at a fairly late date, after the royal family of Jerusalem had been destroyed, to show that the promises to the kings of Israel were actually more deeply rooted than just in the royal family, and that the promises to David could be understood as promises to the ancestor of the whole nation. Thus Abraham became the 'heir' to the royal covenant promises, even though the royal covenant was from a much later period in Israel's history than the original Abraham stories.

Of all the major covenants, we tend to emphasize the one at Sinai, but this covenant did not become important for the people of Israel until quite late in their history. It became the central theme of Deuteronomy, which represents a fairly late and highly developed stage of Israel's theology, even though, as a mark of respect, the laws in it are set in the time of Moses. Deuteronomy constantly reminds the people of the great covenant made at Horeb (the other name for Sinai). The tablets of the Ten Commandments were later kept in the ark of the covenant, and this became the symbol of the nation, and of God's presence with his people. Thus when King David wanted to establish Jerusalem as his new capital city he brought the ark there (2 Sam. 6). This Mosaic covenant was political; it established Israel as a holy nation, God's special possession (Exod. 19.5–6). Entailed in the covenant were the laws which were the laws of the state. It is very hard for us to imagine a regime where all laws are religious laws, but secular law in Israel did not exist. It is this picture of the covenant, which colours most of our thinking about covenant in the Old Testament, and in the expression 'Law and Gospel' it represents the old covenant of the law in contrast with the new covenant of the gospel.

But older than the Mosaic covenant was the royal covenant, which promised stability to the royal house. Most of the accounts of the kings of Israel and Judah come from the hands of those who had developed the newer covenant theology based on the Moses story, and it is hardly surprising that they did not much emphasize the ways which they had outgrown. We therefore find very little about the royal covenant in the history writings of the Old Testament, and we have to piece it together from hints and allusions in the prophets and the psalms. Consequently the picture is not so clear as we should like. This older royal covenant was very similar to the cosmic or eternal covenant which we find in the Similitudes of Enoch. In the Old Testament the royal covenant was associated with the 'anointed one', and with kings who were called the 'sons of God'. This makes it very likely that the cosmic/royal covenant was the background to some parts of the New Testament (e.g. Rom. 8.19: 'creation waits with eager longing for the revealing of the sons of God').

The great oath, the cosmic covenant and the eternal covenant are all the same thing, and we find the ideas in several parts of the Old Testament. Job 38 describes the creation in a very Enochic way. The Lord asks Job: 'who shut in the sea with doors . . . and prescribed bounds for it?' (38.8–10); 'Can you bind the chains of the Pleiades?' (38.31). This is exactly what we find in Enoch; binding the waters and the heavenly bodies. The Prayer of Manasseh in the Apocrypha begins by addressing God as the one who shackled the sea, confined the deep and sealed it with his terrible and glorious name. Here, as in Enoch, it is the power of the name which binds the unruly forces. In these examples we find that the forces of chaos are active not only in the evil angels, with whom we are now familiar, but also in the waters and the deeps. This is a new element in the mythology, not prominent in Enoch, but nevertheless important for understanding some parts of the New Testament. The New Testament also shows us that these royal/cosmic ideas were still associated with the anointed one, the Messiah.

When Jesus stills the storm, the disciples ask: 'What sort of man is this, that even winds and sea obey him?' (Matt. 8.27). When Peter walks on the water, he is successful so long as he has faith (Matt.14.28–30). When the seer John sees the new Jerusalem, the first heaven and the first earth have passed away, and there is no more sea (Rev. 21.1). In all these instances the sea represents what it had represented in the older mythology – chaos, and the forces of evil which threaten the order of creation. Power over the sea, or over the sea monsters who represented the sea, was proof of divine power. Thus Jesus stills the storm, Peter is safe so long as he has faith, and the new creation in Revelation has no more evil. The story of Noah's flood actually describes evil overwhelming itself. The waters were allowed to rise and blot out an evil world.

The psalms are full of pictures of God in triumph over the waters, or rescuing his faithful ones from threat of being overwhelmed by them. Psalm 18.16–17 says the Lord rescues the psalmist from many waters, from strong enemies and those who hate him. Psalm 24.2 says the Lord founded the earth on the seas. Psalm 46 describes the power of God in the midst of roaring waters which symbolize threatening forces; here they are raging nations (Ps. 46.6). Psalm 69 begins: 'Save me, O God! For the waters have come up to my neck.' Psalm 93.4 says the Lord is mightier than the sea. Psalm 104.9 says the Lord has set a bound for the sea, and Psalm 148.6 says the waters above the heavens were fixed with bonds. Job 41 describes Leviathan, the great sea monster whom the Lord has tamed as a sign of his power. The waters which threatened were not the waters of a real sea, although the imagery of subduing the waters could be applied literally, as in Exodus 15.1–18 and Isaiah 51.9–10, which both describe the crossing of the Red Sea in terms of the ancient triumph over the waters. But the sea represented everything terrifying and chaotic, everything which threatened the order of creation. This is why time and again we find that God sets bounds for the sea which it may not pass. They were the sign that the cosmic covenant was secure.

At the centre of the system of control was the Lord's anointed, the king. We see this best in Psalm 89, where the Lord rules the raging sea, stills the waves, crushes the sea monster and scatters enemies, all aspects of the same threat (89.9–10). Then in parallel, as the earthly aspect of the power, we see the king with 'his hand on the sea and his right hand on the rivers' becoming the greatest of all kings (89.25–27). This belief underlies the gospel accounts of Jesus stilling the waves of the storm. There are several later legends about restraining the great flood and all it represents. One in the Babylonian Talmud says that King David suppressed the great flood by writing the name of God on a potsherd, and throwing it into the deep. The power of the name kept the waters in check.

The Old Testament has many examples of the vision of destruction, what happens when the covenant which binds the created order is broken, and things begin to fall apart. It is important to notice that the everlasting covenant does not just bind the natural forces; it also includes moral restraints, and gives us a picture of one law embracing what we might divide into two: natural and moral. One of the best descriptions I have found of this idea comes not from the ancient Near East, but from our Anglo-Saxon ancestors. Brian Bates in his book *The Way of Wyrd* (London, Century 1983) describes their world-view as he has reconstructed it from an ancient manuscript in the British Museum. They had

> a vision of the universe, from the gods to the underworld, as being connected by an enormous all-reaching system of fibres, rather like a three dimensional spider's web. Everything was connected by strands of fibre to the all-encompassing web. This image far surpasses in ambition our present views of ecology, in which we have extended our notions of cause and effect to include longer and more lateral chains of influence in the natural world. The web of fibres of the Anglo-Saxon sorcerer offers an ecological model which encompasses individual life events as well as general physical and biological phenomena, non-material as well as material events, and challenges the very cause and effect chains upon which our ecological theories depend. (p.12)

The image of the web is very powerful, especially when placed in contrast to the linear way of thought, which sees one thing causing another in an endless chain, and one person holding ultimate power. Progress, pilgrimage, getting there and 'making it' are all aspects of this linear view of life. The web view, with everything in all-encompassing interdependence, and several causes and effects in every rupture, whether in the material or non-material world, seems to me to represent more accurately the thought-world of the cosmic covenant. Progress is not seen as the great alteration, exploiting what we have been given (in the angel myth, using the divine knowledge for selfish ends), but rather as the great healing, the great restoration of everything to its own place, not to ours. Another very powerful web picture can be found in Mary Daly's book *Gyn/Ecology* (London, Women's Press 1984). She contrasts the linear, power-seeking view of life with the supportive and creative web view. Being a somewhat angry feminist writer, she associates the linear, power-seeking view with the male world, and finds it symbolized in the great processions by which statements of status are made: processions of clergy, academics, judges. She calls on spinsters to spin a new web and renew the world, to see progress as healing, and to feel the mutual 'interbeing' of all things.

Some of the prophetic pictures of the broken covenant speak directly to our age of ecological crisis. Isaiah 24.4–6 sees heaven and earth withering. Note the parallel, as above, so below:

> The earth mourns and withers,
> the world languishes and withers;
> the heavens languish together with the earth.
> The earth lies polluted
> under its inhabitants;
> for they have transgressed the laws,
> violated the statutes,
> broken the everlasting covenant.
> Therefore a curse devours the earth,
> and its inhabitants suffer for their guilt;
> therefore the inhabitants of the earth are scorched,
> and few men are left.

This is the same picture as Enoch's, and the pattern continues to correspond. In Enoch the broken covenant leads to the judgement; here in Isaiah 24.21–22 the broken covenant leads to the judgement:

> On that day the Lord will punish
> the host of heaven, in heaven,
> and the kings of the earth, on the earth.
> They will be gathered together
> as prisoners in a pit;
> they will be shut up in a prison,
> and after many days they will be punished.

Isaiah 33.7–9 also deals with the broken covenant. All the characters mentioned are angel figures according to the Jewish tradition – valiant ones, envoys of peace (better 'angels of peace'; they are the same words), witnesses. The covenants are broken and the land withers. There are similar pictures at Hosea 2.18, a covenant with the beasts of the field; at Jeremiah 33.19–22, where God promises that the covenant with David will be as stable as the covenant with the day and the night; at Ezekiel 34.25, the covenant of peace which brings fertility and safety. When the covenant is broken, powerful destructive forces are released and the creation is at risk.

We see another picture of this in Joel. Evil enemies had come against the land (2:2):

> Like blackness there is spread upon the mountains
> a great and powerful people;
> their like has never been from of old
> nor will be again after them
> through the years of all generations

and the land itself had ceased to bear food (1:17):

> The seed shrivels under the clods,
> the storehouses are desolate;
> the granaries are ruined
> because the grain has failed.

These are two aspects of the broken covenant: attack from enemies and failure of the world of nature. We think of the disasters of war and the disasters of famine in separate categories, but the prophet saw both as aspects of the broken covenant. The oracles were delivered in the hot summer months of drought, the period before the autumn festival when Israel usually celebrated both the harvest and the triumph of her God and king over her enemies. But that year there was no triumph, and no harvest. Joel described the mourning and repentance for the broken covenant. We find the familiar words: 'Rend your hearts and not your garments' (Joel 2.13). We find the promise that all would be restored in words that are equally familiar: 'I will pour out my spirit on all flesh' (Joel 2.28). The great covenant was to be restored; the earth was to regain its fertility, and the people of God were to be saved from their enemies, from the evil forces which had broken the cosmic covenant. It was this passage in Joel which inspired Peter's great Pentecost sermon (Acts 2.14–36). This shows us that the giving of the Spirit and the birth of the Church were closely bound up with Joel's vision of a renewal of the cosmic covenant, the restoration of all creation. Perhaps we should hear more about this in our Whitsun sermons. Our poets and artists are still describing the broken covenant; Yeats saw all too clearly the dissolution of the created order in 'The Second Coming':

> Things fall apart; the centre cannot hold;
> Mere anarchy is loosed upon the world,

The blood-dimmed tide is loosed, and everywhere
The ceremony of innocence is drowned.

The apocalyptic tradition, which was the mother of Christianity, preserved the idea of the cosmic covenant, the judgement, and the great renewal. But it always had a vision beyond the end; we call it life after death.

The main figure in the eternal covenant was the king, the earthly agent of the Lord. He it was who kept the forces of evil at bay. We have already mentioned Psalm 89, which shows the king in this role; to this must be added Psalm 2, where the rulers of the earth plot against the Lord and his anointed to break out of their bonds; Psalm 72, which links the king's justice to the fertility of the land; and Isaiah 11, which depicts the messianic king who will bring justice and judgement, followed by harmony in the creation. The passage ends, significantly, 'They shall not hurt or destroy in all my holy mountain' (Isa. 11.9). As above, so below.

Compare this ancient picture of creation with that in Genesis; Enoch's is probably the older picture. Genesis 1 offers several hints that it replaced an older account; certainly it is very different from the picture of binding and restraining evil forces. Genesis 1 gives a picture of ordered calm. God commands, and it is done. The waters separate and the firmament appears. There is no hint of shackling a hostile sea or prescribing its limits. Wherever the Genesis meditation on the nature of the world originated, it reflects a relatively late view of the creation. It was not until the time of the second temple that there was great emphasis on separation from other nations in order to keep a national identity, yet here in Genesis 1 we find separation perceived as one of the principles of creation. Everything is separated, each according to its kind. And the great threats of the older systems are made passive; the waters separate at God's command, the lights of heaven are simply to distinguish day and night, and the great sea monsters are created along with all other animal life. This later idea of the creation is the one we tend to bring to the whole of the Old Testament and the New, yet it does not offer us any background to Romans 8, nor does it explain how that obedient creation which God saw as good became the demon-infested place of the Gospels. Nowhere is the older account of the creation ever spelt out in the Old Testament. Thus it has been overlooked. We have to pick up what hints we can in the prophets and the psalms, and in the books which are not in the Old Testament. But the hints do fit into a coherent picture of a more violent creation, where hostile forces were restrained by the power of God. Enoch's two short pieces on the great oath are the best extended account that we have.

The binding of evil has a place in the New Testament. Casting out demons requires that the strong one be bound first (Matt.12.29). Peter, having recognized Jesus as the Messiah, is given the power to bind and to loose both in heaven and on earth (Matt. 16.13–19). There are several similarities between this story of Peter's commission and Enoch's. (Both happen in the same place, for example.) The most likely explanation of Peter's commission is that he was given power over the evil ones (cf. Luke 10.17, where demons are subjected in Jesus' name, and note the role of the *name* in the task of binding). The power given to Peter (symbolized by the keys of the kingdom of heaven which now form the papal coat of arms) was later interpreted as the power to bind and loose sins, the power to absolve. The roots of the idea, however, lie not in forgiving the sin committed by human beings, but in protecting them from evil done to them. The binding was the restraining of evil forces.

This binding of evil spirits to restore the creation is barely distinguishable from the practice of magic, by which is meant not the music-hall tricks of a modern magician, but the more serious practices of dealing with illness and possession. Witch doctors, or perhaps faith healers, are the nearest equivalent we have today. In the ancient world there were many magicians who exorcized as Jesus did, and it is not surprising that non-Christian writers often described Jesus as a magician. The early Church was at pains to separate itself from these people, but the lines were not always distinctly drawn. In addition, the New Testament was written at a time when it was important that the distinction be maintained, and it is quite likely that any ambiguous evidence has been excluded from the accounts. Even so, we have a picture of the early problems. Simon Magus (i.e. Simon the Magician) in Samaria tried to buy the Christian secret (Acts 8.14–24). Elymas the magician in Cyprus, who came into conflict with Paul, was a Jewish false prophet (Acts 13.4–12). The account of Paul's time in Ephesus (Acts 19.11–20) shows that itinerant Jewish exorcists were using the name of Jesus in their craft, and, although the text is not entirely clear, verses 18–19 do seem to be saying that many who had become Christians continued with their magical arts until persuaded not to.

Christians were noted as healers, even after the apostolic age. There

is a story told of a Christian in Galilee in the early first century, Jacob
of Sana. He was summoned by a rabbi (!) who had been bitten by a
snake. Another rabbi forbade him to be healed by a Christian. The
success of the Christians led to the name of Jesus being used in spells,
alongside those of Abraham, Isaac, Jacob, Moses, and even versions
of the sacred name of God. Here are extracts from one well-known
spell from the *Great Magical Papyrus* (now in the Bibliothèque
Nationale in Paris) showing us the world of Enoch's great oath and of
the Christian healings:

An approved recipe of Pibekeus against those possessed of a demon

Take unripe olives and mastyx plant, and lotos and boil it together
with wild marjoram.
Place thyself before the possessed and conjure:
I conjure thee in the name of the God of the Hebrews IAOO.
I conjure thee whatever spirit or demon thou mayest be, speak,
for I conjure thee with the seal which Solomon placed upon
the mouth of Jeremia.
I conjure thee with him who has made the sand to be as a wall of
mountains around the sea, and has bound it not to pass
beyond it and the sea obeyed.
I conjure thee with the holy name of the One who dwells in the
pure Jerusalem.
The conjuror must blow from the lower extremities upwards
until he reaches the face, and the demon will be driven out. Keep
clean and pure, for this conjuration is Hebrew, and is preserved
by pure men.

Notice the name of God, a garbled version of the Hebrew divine name
Yahweh; the seal of Solomon; the obedience of the sea, and the
necessity for ritual purity.

We are not in a position to know how far early Christian thinking
was influenced by the idea of the cosmic covenant. There is very little
about the creation in the New Testament, and we have tended to draw
on the picture in Genesis as the sole 'biblical' basis of our ideas. We do
know, however, that the early Christians knew and used the book of
Enoch. The cosmic covenant passages are in that section of Enoch for
which we have no proof of a pre-Christian date, and this again must
make us cautious. Nevertheless, there is sufficient in the Old Testament to enable us to reconstruct the cosmic covenant in outline, and

this fits so well with the picture in Enoch that we shall not be too far wide of the mark if we take that as a possible background to the New Testament.

The most important passage dealing with creation is Romans 8.14–23. Paul says that we are sons of God (a name pointing us to the angels) because we have received the spirit of sonship. In the account of the fallen angels in Genesis 6 (which is very confused) the result of the sin is that the spirit of the Lord 'shall not abide in man for ever'. Paul reverses this and links the giving of the Spirit with acquiring the status of sonship. Creation waits for the revealing of the sons of God, so that it may be released from bondage to decay. The subjection of creation was the will of God, says Paul, and it is also one of the inexplicable aspects of the apocalyptists' world-view that God permits suffering. (The alternative would be to say he was powerless to prevent it, given that suffering exists, and this they would not say.) The evil shepherds in the Book of Dreams were permitted to harm the people of God up to a certain point, and in the Book of the Watchers the evil demons were permitted to infest the earth until the time came for their judgement. The new sons of God would be the means of undoing the work of the former, fallen sons. We can see the process of reversal at work in the earliest Christian thinking. The Spirit returns and makes new sons of God. They regain the immortality and access to heaven which the first sons of God forfeited by their disobedience, and the creation is restored to its true state of joy. According to Enoch, it is the name and the power of the Son of Man which makes this judgement effective.

The language of binding and restraining is very evocative. We often speak of harnessing or unleashing powerful forces. The greatest breaking of bonds in our own time must surely have been the discovery of nuclear power. The official report sent to President Truman after the first atom bomb was exploded in New Mexico was in apocalyptic terms: 'Then came the strong, sustained, awesome roar which warned of doomsday and made us feel that we puny things were blasphemous to dare to tamper with the forces heretofore reserved to the Almighty.' Nicholas Humphrey's Bronowski Memorial Lecture 'Four Minutes to Midnight' published in *The Listener*, 29 August 1981, which caused such a furore, analysed people's reactions to this enormous force which has been unleashed. Although he was probably unaware of it, Humphrey too used the language of the apocalyptists to describe the psychological state of people overtaken by evil – blindness:

And in the face of this knowledge we may find ourselves suffering from another kind of blindness, a blindness equally human, but in many ways less innocent than the blindness that comes from lack of understanding. I mean the deliberate blindness which comes over us when we see something and then reject it: when we recognise the truth or at least part of the truth, and – finding it perhaps too painful or inconvenient – censor its access to our conscious minds. I mean what psychologists have called Denial.

This is exactly how Enoch sees a world where the cosmic covenant is broken. Rebel angels, figures of great power, brought knowledge to earth which corrupted and destroyed the creation. The rebel angels had knowledge of technology, medicine and the arts of communication. They were incarnate in political leaders, and those who came under their influence became blind. In his vision Enoch saw the Son of Man restoring the great bonds of creation, healing the rift between earth and heaven, and thus restoring the earth. In less mythological language, we might say bringing beliefs and values into a scientific society which are neither derived from it nor limited by it.

The miracle of healing in John 9 shows how deeply this world-view permeates the Gospels. A man had been born blind, not because of any sin, but so that the power of God could be shown. Jesus healed him. When his eyes were opened, people were wary of him because Jesus did not have the authentication of the establishment. Jesus asked the blind man if he believed in the Son of Man. Why should Jesus have asked about the Son of Man when there had been a healing of blindness? If we read the Fourth Gospel in the light of 1 Enoch and its theology, we realize that the ending of blindness was a sign that the power of evil was being broken and the cosmic covenant was being restored. This was the role of the Son of Man.

Chapter 7

The Son of Man

Who or what was the Son of Man? In later Christian usage 'Son of Man' and 'Son of God' stood for the human and the divine in Jesus; Son of Man was the human aspect, Son of God the divine. Yet here in the Similitudes of Enoch, Son of Man is clearly the name used for a heavenly figure, not a human being. This is the first Son of Man problem: Which meaning was the one intended by the gospel writers? The second problem is whether or not the phrase originally referred to Jesus. In the Gospels as we now have them, Son of Man does refer to Jesus. But was this a later development of Christian thinking, and not a part of Jesus' own description of himself? In some of the sayings it could conceivably be referring to someone else. For example, in Mark 14.61–62 the High Priest asks: 'Are you the Christ, the Son of the Blessed?' and Jesus replies: 'I am; and you will see the Son of man seated at the right hand of Power . . .' If we cannot prove that being the Christ, the Son of the Blessed, was the same as being the Son of Man (i.e. if we cannot prove that Son of Man was associated with the Messiah), then it is just possible that Jesus was referring to someone other than himself at the right hand of God. The answer to this question is very important in helping us understand how Jesus saw himself, because the phrase Son of Man is used in the Gospels in the sayings of Jesus, and seems to have been characteristic of him. Did he say these things about himself (i.e. was he the Son of Man), or did he refer to another as Son of Man? And was 'son of man' just the phrase for a human being, as later usage implied, or was it an angelic title, as Enoch suggests?

There has been a long debate around these possibilities, and the various positions have been expressed in several ways. In a nutshell, the argument goes like this (bearing in mind that any simplification has to sacrifice some of the subtleties of the debate):

'Son of Man' can exist with or without the article – i.e. as *the* Son of Man, or as *a* Son of Man. (I shall omit the arguments about the differences between these two, since they require a knowledge of Aramaic and Greek, but it is important to know that the two forms do exist. 'A Son of Man' implies that there could be more than one of them, whereas '*the* Son of Man' sounds rather more emphatic and exclusive. In either form it is very unusual Greek, and consequently stands awkwardly in the New Testament. Even the way we write the phrase suggests how we have understood it, or wish it to be understood. Does it have capital letters or not? Was it just a noun, or was it a title?)

It is suggested that this phrase came originally from an Aramaic phrase, *bar enash*, literally 'son of man', but in fact used in everyday speech to mean simply a man, when referring to oneself. It would have corresponded to the English usage 'one does so and so . . .' If it does mean just 'a man', this would account for the later custom of using it for the human nature of Jesus. There are several places in the Gospels where this suggestion fits well. 'Foxes have holes, and birds of the air have nests; but the Son of man has nowhere to lay his head' (Matt. 8.20, Luke 9.58) makes sense as Jesus talking about himself, and his way of life; it does not imply any angelic being. There are also places where the words of Jesus are reported in two different ways. For example, Matthew 10.32 says: 'So every one who acknowledges me before men, I also will acknowledge before my Father who is in heaven', whereas the parallel saying in Luke 12.8 is: 'And I tell you, every one who acknowledges me before men, the Son of man also will acknowledge before the angels of God'. Mark 8.38 is similar: 'For whoever is ashamed of me . . . of him will the Son of man also be ashamed, when he comes in the glory of his Father with the holy angels.' This implies that 'I' and 'the Son of Man' were understood by the gospel writers to have the same meaning. But if Jesus thought of himself as an angelic figure, one sent from God, 'I' and 'Son of Man' could still be interchanged and yet allow for 'Son of Man' to imply an angelic figure. This argument is not without problems.

The curious form of the phrase 'son of man' can be understood from the common custom of Semitic languages such as Hebrew and Aramaic. 'Son of' did not only mean being someone's son; it could also describe someone's characteristics, or the group to which one belonged. Thus in 2 Kings 2.3 'the sons of the prophets' does not mean the families of the prophets, but rather the community, those who belonged to that group of prophets. 'A son of man' would have meant just a member of the human race, as we can see in the similar use of the Hebrew *ben*, 'son', in the Old Testament. A clear example is Psalm 144.3:

> O Lord, what is man that thou dost regard him,
> or the son of man that thou dost think of him?

The poetry of this psalm has pairs of lines with parallel meanings, therefore 'man' and 'son of man' must have been equivalent. There are similar phrases in Psalms 31.19; 33.13; 57.4.

The gist of the remainder of this argument is that when the earliest Christians were reflecting on the life and teaching of Jesus, after they had realized who he was, they took the phrase he so often used when referring impersonally to himself as a human being, 'son of man', and linked it to the most famous of all the 'Son of Man' passages in the Old Testament, Daniel 7.13. The sayings of Jesus which speak of a Son of Man like the one in Daniel's vision, the human agent of the great judgement coming with clouds and angels, are then said to be derived from Daniel 7, as part of the early Church's development of its picture of Christ. This creative theologizing fashioned sayings which were then put into the mouth of Jesus by the gospel writers, or by the communities whose traditions they recorded, because they felt that they were true to their understanding of Jesus, even if they had not been part of Jesus' understanding of himself.

The process happened in two stages. At first Jesus was described as in Daniel 7, not as '*the* Son of Man', a title, but as 'one like a son of man' (i.e. one like a human being, which is what Daniel actually says), who was exalted to the presence of God. Gradually 'one like a son of man' became a title, 'the Son of Man' and Daniel was used as the pattern to fill in details of Jesus as the heavenly judge. There is, say supporters of this view, no evidence that 'Son of Man' was used as a title, let alone as a messianic title, in New Testament times. It means simply 'a man' and all the rest came from the growth of tradition within the Church. The role of Jesus in the future judgement could not possibly have been depicted in any other way. Existing expectations of judgement had to be modified to include Jesus, and thus the Son of Man sayings came about. This is crucial to the argument for this position, but unfortunately, as we shall see later, there is a considerable amount of indirect evidence to associate 'Son of Man' with the Messiah, and therefore a good case for seeing 'the Son of Man' as more than a figure of speech, and for using the Son of Man figure in Enoch as background to the New Testament.

The alternative view is that 'Son of Man', whether or not it was a title, did have some significance, that it meant more than 'I', that it was used by Jesus to describe himself, and that he knew the significance of what he was saying. He was associating himself with an angelic emissary of the judgement. The variations which are apparent in the Gospels could be due to the hazards of oral transmission, and not to the wholesale manufacture of a new theology. The Similitudes of Enoch give the clearest picture of a supernatural Son of Man figure, but they have never been admitted as evidence in the New Testament debate because there is no proof that they are a pre-Christian text. I should like to approach this Enochic material in another way, and not simply say, 'Is this text pre- or post-Christian?' I suggest that the factors which are presently used in both sides of this debate can be used together to answer the question, 'Who is the Son of Man?' In order to do this we have to range widely to collect the evidence.

First, it is true that we have no evidence that the Similitudes are pre-Christian, but it is possible to make a good case for their roots and the ideas in them being pre-Christian. If we read Isaiah 1–39 we find that the themes of the prophet are remarkably like those of Enoch. Their thought-worlds were the same. I am not saying that the two books are identical, because they are not, but that their authors used the same mental framework in order to communicate. We have already seen how the call vision in Isaiah 6 is very similar to Enoch's, and how Isaiah 24–7 and Isaiah 33 are very Enochic, with their angels and judgement themes. Isaiah, like Enoch, has no real place for the Moses and Exodus theology, but there is great emphasis on judgement (Isa. 2.12–21; 5.13–17; 14; 19; 22; 24–7; 34, etc.), the sin of pride (Isa. 14; 37.23–29), angels of judgement (Isa. 37.36–38), the angel mythology (Isa. 14; 24.21–22) and the restoration of creation (Isa. 35). Isaiah's was the world of the first temple, the world in which the Enochic writings claim to have had their roots. Those who built the second temple, say the Enochic writings, were impure and apostate. It is curious that all these themes from Isaiah are also prominent in Enoch. 1 Enoch does not quote Isaiah or in any way use the book as a source. It is possible therefore that both 1 Enoch and Isaiah come from the same stratum of Israel's history and theology. The one major theme of Isaiah which is not in the pre-Christian Enoch texts at Qumran is the theme of the royal figure. Isaiah 9 and 11 both depict a heavenly royal figure who was wise and divine (9.6), who would rule on the throne of David (9.7), and who would establish justice and cosmic harmony (11.3–9). The royal figure in Isaiah, which the Christians took to be a prophetic prediction of Jesus, is exactly like the figure we find in the Similitudes. The Similitudes describe him in much more detail, but the basic royal/angelic figure who brings judgement is the same. I suggest, therefore, that although there is no proof that the Similitudes are pre-Christian, the judgement theme of the Similitudes is an important part of that earlier theology to which the rest of Enoch bears such a strong resemblance, and which we find as a coherent whole in the First Isaiah. The heavenly judgement figure may have been developed and elaborated by later generations, but it was not actually invented by them, nor was it alien to the Enochic tradition. The roots of the figure in the Similitudes are as old as the traditions in Isaiah.

Second, we know that the pre-Christian parts of Enoch had a peculiar code. We do not know why they had it, but only that they did have it. They described angel figures as men or men in white. This is not an isolated usage, in fact it occurs several times. In 1 Enoch 87.2 we read that beings like white men came from heaven; they were the archangels. In 1 Enoch 89.36 a sheep became a man, meaning that a human being had achieved angelic status. In 1 Enoch 90.14,22 the heavenly scribe at the great judgement is a man. Cf. also 1 Enoch 93.4, 5, 8, the three cases in the Apocalypse of Weeks where human beings become angelic; they are then described as men. 'Man' in Enoch can refer either to an angel, or to a human being who achieves the heavenly angelic state. Now the debate about 'son of man' has concluded from a study of Aramaic usage that 'son of man' only means man. Thus in Daniel 7 'one like a son of man' is only a human figure. But in Enoch 'men' are archangels. It is therefore likely that an angelic vision in Daniel will have used similar terminology. 'A man' was an angel figure, or one who had become angelic. The Enochic Book of Dreams, where these 'men' occur most frequently, was written at about the same time as Daniel, during the crisis which led to the Maccabean revolt. It is unlikely that the meanings in Enoch and Daniel were totally different. The figure in Daniel's vision, the 'man', must have been an angel, but since he went to the throne we may perhaps assume that he was like one of Enoch's human beings who became 'men'. In other words, the son of man figure was a human being who became divine and was given dominion. Like Enoch, Daniel also has animals; in his vision they are the four fearful beasts who represent the four empires. In Revelation there are also beasts, and son of man figures who are angelic; Revelation 1.13 describes 'one like a son of man', and Revelation 14.14 'a son of man, with a golden crown on his head, and a sharp sickle in his hand'. 'A son of man', or a man, meant an angelic figure. We must not read the biblical apocalypses on their own. 1 Enoch, and works like it, must fill in the details.

Third, this strange use of 'man' was not restricted to the apocalyptists. By New Testament times there had already grown up among Jewish interpreters the belief that 'man' in the Scriptures could be a secret reference to the Messiah. The Targum (commentary) to Psalm 80.17 applies

> But let thy hand be upon the man of thy right hand,
> the son of man whom thou hast made strong for thyself!

to the Messiah. Zechariah 6.12, 'Behold, the man whose name is the Branch', was thought to refer to the Messiah, and the repeated promise to the royal house (1 Kings 2.4; 8.25; 9.5, etc.) that there would always be a man to sit on the throne strengthened this association of the 'man' and the royal house. Daniel 7 had also become associated with the Messiah by New Testament times, and although the Son of Man was not a title as such, the phrase had strong messianic associations. For example, there was a play written at the end of the second century BC by one Ezekiel (not the prophet, but another of the same name). In the play Moses dreams that he sees a great throne. The man on the throne summons Moses to ascend, gives him a crown, and invites him to sit on another throne. This is the same sequence of events as in Daniel 7, but with the additional detail that Moses is made a king and given a crown. This shows that he was made king Messiah when he ascended. Since this is what a Son of Man did in the almost contemporary vision of Daniel, that vision too must have had messianic associations.

We have therefore three independent pieces of evidence to bring to our understanding of the phrase 'Son of Man' in the New Testament: first, that the royal figure in the Similitudes is quite at home in the pre-Christian Enochic theology, even though there are no pre-Christian texts of the Similitudes; second, that the apocalyptists used 'man' to mean an angel figure; and, third, that by New Testament times 'man' had messianic associations, as did Daniel 7. It is therefore unlikely that Jesus used the phrase 'Son of Man' with no messianic or angelic overtones, and that he used it to mean simply a man, a human being. The early Church may have elaborated some of the sayings in the course of transmission, and even added some of its own making; but I doubt that there was any fundamental change from the intention of Jesus himself. 'Son of Man' is therefore very important for our understanding of the New Testament, since it is our way into seeing how Jesus understood his role and his mission.

If we use the picture of the Son of Man in Enoch, we have a rough guide as to what was implicit in the New Testament. The Son of Man is the heavenly pattern, the heavenly counterpart to a person on earth who fulfils the same role. Notice that it is *a* person, not *the* person. Several people had already been called to this task; Ezekiel was commissioned to announce judgement, as were Enoch and Jesus. They were deemed angelic figures by virtue of their heavenly role. They had visions. They were agents of God. Thus John 5.27 says God has given Jesus authority to execute judgement because he is Son of Man (there is no 'the' in the Greek), Matthew also shows us the old belief that the anointed king was God's agent; he rephrases several passages, and instead of 'God' writes 'Son of Man'. Thus in Mark 9.1 we have 'the kingdom of God', which is paralleled in Matthew 16.28 by 'the kingdom of the Son of man'. The Son of man was the agent and visible manifestation of God. In the parable of the sheep and the goats, the Son of Man is the king who sits in judgement (Matt. 25.31,34), a sure sign that the Son of Man had royal connections.

In the Similitudes we have the most detailed account of what the Son of Man was and did. In the first Similitude he dwells under the wings of the Lord of Spirits. This is a memory of the great royal throne in the temple, which was flanked by the wings of cherubim. In his days justice is established; the great judgement takes place before him, just as it had been enacted in the ancient temple rituals. In the second Similitude we learn that the Elect One will sit on the throne of judgement, the earth will be transformed, and the elect ones will live there. The Son of Man stands by the Ancient of Days, and the angel reveals that he will be the judge of the kings and the mighty. The words are reminiscent of the Magnificat. What can have inspired this ancient Christian canticle? A similar expectation of judgement? Why was it attributed to Mary? If it really was associated with her, or the expectations of people of her background, then was an Enochic expectation of the judgement part of the environment in which Jesus grew up? These are all speculations, but they are questions to make us stop and think. What did influence the way Jesus saw himself and his role? Could he himself have been influenced in his thinking by the very texts which we usually assume were the source of the later Christian community's elaborated picture of him?

Enoch then sees a vision of the fountains of wisdom, and hears the name of the Son of Man, the name which preceded the creation:

Yea, before the sun and the signs were created,
Before the stars of the heaven were made,
His name was named before the Lord of Spirits.   (1 Enoch 48.3)

On the day of judgement all who have denied the Lord and his anointed will fall and never rise again. The Elect One stands before the Lord, filled with the spirit of wisdom and insight (the words are reminiscent of Isa. 11). He sits on the throne revealing the secrets of wisdom. The creation rejoices, the angels are filled with joy; great mountains melt at his feet. A part of the punishment of the kings and the mighty is that they will recognize the Elect One before he condemns them. The third Similitude describes the Elect One on the throne, judging heaven and earth. The Lord of Spirits summons all the angels and powers, and among these is the Elect One. They all join in a great song of praise. Again the kings and mighty are required to recognize the Elect One, to understand who he is. The Son of Man has been hidden, and revealed only to the chosen. Finally the power of the cosmic oath is strengthened with the Name of the Son of Man, and the creation is rebound and renewed.

The Similitudes are confused; it seems as though the texts have been dislocated in the course of transmission, and we have snippets about the Son of Man/Elect One scattered throughout. Several themes emerge: he is an angelic figure who sits on the throne of judgement; he has been hidden, perhaps this means not recognized by the kings and the mighty; his name is a powerful force for healing and restoring the creation; he is the source of wisdom; he is the anointed one. At first sight it seems unlikely that these elaborate pictures have any bearing upon the New Testament, but in fact there are significant correspondences. The first Christians often described Jesus as an angel figure, as did the demons whom he drove out – 'I know who you are, the Holy One of God' (Mark 1.24). Jesus as the agent of God's judgement is a major theme of the Fourth Gospel (John 5.27; 8.16; 12.47). The secret of the Messiah, his hiddenness, is a major theme of Mark (Mark 1.44; 3.12; 5.83; 8.22–26); cf. the pre-Christian tradition that Enoch was hidden: 'Before these things Enoch was hidden, and no one of the children of men knew where he was hidden, and where he abode, and what had become of him. And his activities had to do with the Watchers, and his days were with the holy ones' (1 Enoch 12.1–2).

And there are also the later legends of the hidden Enoch (see p. 1). The rulers of the time did not recognize Jesus. The 'name' of Jesus was the means of healing and exorcising (e.g. Luke 10.17). This degree of correspondence suggests that a figure like Enoch's Son of Man was in the gospel writers' minds as they compiled their accounts, even in passages where the actual phrase 'Son of Man' does not occur.

One of the assumptions often made is that the Son of Man in Daniel was the original, the one source of all other references to the Son of Man or even to ascents and heavenly enthronements. The writer of Daniel 7, it is implied, wrote something entirely new and unheard-of when he described his vision of 'one like a son of man'. If Daniel 7 is the source of all the later pictures, then where these differ we have to say that Daniel 7 has been altered, modified, corrupted. If, however, Daniel 7 was a vision based on well-known ideas (as visions often are), it may be that Daniel 7 and several other Son of Man visions can all contribute equally valuable information about the mysterious figure, and point us to the source of all of them.

There is a man vision in 2 Esdras 13. After sitting seven days in a field, eating only plants and flowers, Ezra has a vision of a rough sea. This is exactly how the great vision of Daniel 7 begins, with a beast rising from the sea. Daniel sees four terrible beasts in the first part of the vision. In 2 Esdras 12. 11 Ezra has already seen a vision of a monster which the angel interpreter said was the fourth of Daniel's beasts. We are therefore expecting Ezra's vision to relate to the final part of Daniel's. The wind causes something like the figure of a man to come from the sea and fly with clouds. His gaze and voice are terrible, melting everything before him like wax. Next Ezra sees a huge multitude coming against the man, who carves a great mountain for himself and flees to it. From this vantage point the man defeats the hordes with a stream of fire from his mouth. He then comes down from the mountain to greet another crowd who have come in peace, bringing offerings. An interpretation of the vision is given: the man is one who has been kept hidden (NB) by the Most High, destined to liberate the creation. Various details are worked out, but the impression given is that we have a passage which has had several additions, some of them Christian, but all of them are finding significance in a vision which was itself older than any of the attempts to interpret it. Ezra's man and Daniel's figure 'like a son of man' were the same, and both Ezra and Daniel gave different versions of one underlying mythology.

The Son of Man vision in Daniel 7 describes four fearful beasts coming from the sea, followed by one 'like a son of man'. Daniel does not say where the Son of Man figure comes from; we are only told that he went with clouds to the Ancient of Days, where he was given dominion and glory and kingdom. The interpretation of the vision (Dan. 7.27) says that the son of man figure represents the whole people of God in their eventual triumph; but this is the interpretation of the vision, and not necessarily the explanation of its original form. Artists and visionaries do not create the mythology they interpret. There is yet another man vision in 2 Esdras 2.42ff, the passage used in the Anglican lectionary for All Saints' Day. This time Ezra sees a very tall young man (angels were often thought of as very tall), giving crowns to a great multitude on Mount Zion. The angel interpreter tells Ezra that these people have put on the clothing of immortality; the young man is the Son of God who gives them crowns and palms. This is the same picture as in Revelation 7.9–10, the multitude in white robes with palm branches in their hands; and in Hebrews 12.22–24, the festal gathering in heavenly Jerusalem. The key to the origin of all these vivid images is the palm branches, as we shall see later.

We are looking for a situation in which a son of man figure came from the water, went up with clouds to the great throne, sat in judgement and was surrounded by people waving palm branches on Mount Zion. We are looking for a great festival gathering in Jerusalem, or the memory of it, which could have been the source of all these images in Daniel, 2 Esdras, Enoch and Revelation. Here we find ourselves confronted with a familiar problem: the Old Testament does not answer all the questions we should like to put to it. We have to piece together what we can.

The major theme of the son of man texts is judgement. If we look at other references to judgement in the biblical texts, we find the recurring theme of a great harvest. Amos 8.1–3 is the earliest, the picture of the summer fruit. 'Summer fruit' and 'end' sound very similar in Hebrew, and Amos associates the fruit harvest with a prophecy of judgement. Jeremiah sees judgement as the grim reaper (Jer. 9.21). Isaiah gave us the original grapes of wrath trampled by God at the great judgement (Isa. 63.1–6). There is the preaching of John the Baptist, judgement as threshing and gathering (Matt. 3.12), and the gospel parables of harvest and judgement (e.g. Matt. 13.24–43, esp. vv. 37–42). There is the fearful imagery of the angel reapers, and the angels who gather the grapes of wickedness to press in the winepress of wrath (Rev. 14.14–20). This suggests that judgement, or the liturgical representation of it, was associated with the harvest time. We cannot say that one judgement passage with harvest imagery has been copied by another, because there are so many different aspects of harvest represented. We can only conclude that it was the whole theme of harvest which was associated with judgement. The palm branches carried by the great multitudes in the visions of the judgement confirm this, because the great harvest festival of Israel, the feast of Sukkoth (also called Booths, Tabernacles, and Tents) was celebrated by building leafy shelters and carrying branches in a great procession. (Neh. 8.13–18 describes a celebration in Nehemiah's time.)

The second stage of the reconstruction shows how the harvest/ judgement festival was associated with the royal figure and his ascending the throne. This whole area is full of problems, and scholars cannot even begin to agree. What follows is but an attempt to fit the evidence into some sort of framework. Zechariah 14 is that prophet's description of 'the day of the Lord' (the day of judgement). He associates the day of judgement with the Lord becoming king over the whole earth (Zech. 14.9), and all nations coming to Jerusalem to keep the feast of Sukkoth and to worship the king. In other words, harvest was the time of coronation ritual as well as judgement. We find this pattern in several psalms. (Any use of the psalms is difficult, because we do not know their original use and setting; we have to guess, and admit that one informed guess is as good as any other.) Psalms 46–48 probably belong to this setting. Psalm 46 describes the triumph of God over enemies and waters; Psalm 47, which became the traditional psalm of New Year's Day (the Autumn Festival), describes the Lord as king, sitting on the great throne; Psalm 48 describes the power of the great king, the judge of those who come against him. Psalms 96–99 extol the kingship of God: 'The Lord reigns' (Pss. 96.10; 97.1; 99.1). This is the same imagery as we find in the Son of Man visions; the earth trembles, creation rejoices at the judgement, fire and lightnings surround the throne, mountains melt like wax. There are other echoes of the old ceremony in Deuteronomy 33.2–29, where the coming of the Lord is described. He appears ('dawns', 'shines' – the old imagery of the sun) with all his holy ones, gives the Law and becomes king (Deut. 33.5). The text is not easy to read, but what we can recover shows us that it is exactly like the opening chapters of Enoch, which describe the coming of the Great Holy One with his angels on the day of judgement. Harvest, judgement and coronation therefore belonged together in the most ancient stratum of Israel's religion. The young man distributing crowns and palms was acting out an ancient pattern.

But, it will be objected, these biblical passages all describe how the Lord became king. They do not mention the Son of Man or even the earthly king. Here we must return to the evidence from the Similitudes, and their pattern of correspondences, and use this to read more carefully some Old Testament texts. In the world of the first temple in Jerusalem, the Lord was the Holy One, the guardian angel of Israel, and his earthly representative was the king. We see this is the pattern of Psalm 89, where God and king function in parallel, and especially in Psalm 2, often described as a coronation psalm. This psalm is an earlier representation of the imagery of Daniel 7. The kings of the earth come against the Lord and his anointed (Ps. 2.2), but the anointed is set firm on the holy hill, and the hostile kings are warned to subject themselves to the Lord. In 2 Esdras this element appears as the hostile mob, and in Daniel's vision the kings of the earth are represented by the four beasts, using the animal symbolism which we find in Enoch. The safeguard against all these horrors is the Lord's king set on Zion, the son of the Lord, the one to subdue and break hostile forces. We see this in Psalm 110, another royal psalm: 'Sit at my right hand, till I make your enemies your footstool' (Ps. 110.1). On the day he is made king the Lord says to him: 'You are my son, today I have begotten you' (Ps. 2.7), and from that time forward the king is treated as the Lord, and accepted as his earthly manifestation. In 1 Chronicles 29.20,23 we have a rare glimpse of the ancient kings, but unfortunately the English translations obscure the vital point and are not true to the Hebrew. 1 Chronicles 29.20 actually says: 'They bowed their heads and worshipped the Lord and the king' (i.e. they worshipped the king as well as the Lord, who was his heavenly counterpart). 1 Chronicles 29.23 says that Solomon 'sat on the throne of the Lord as king'. In other words, the king was the visible manifestation of the presence of the Lord. It is this belief which is the ultimate origin of the saying in the Fourth Gospel: 'I and the Father are one [thing]'.

In the Similitudes we see three separate memories of the ancient ceremony of enthronement, with the angelic figure of the king acting as agent of God's judgement. It was ideas of the Son of Man like these which were in the minds of the New Testament writers as they wrote. We cannot say that the Similitudes were their source, because there is no proof of this, but the Son of Man imagery was so widely used, and in such a variety of ways, that it would be very difficult to imagine how Jesus could not have known it. We sadly impoverish our understanding of his ministry if we dismiss the Son of Man sayings as a later addition. Whether or not 'Son of Man' was a distinct title in New Testament times is not known, but 'Son of Man' certainly meant an angelic figure. If we collect all the fragments of Son of Man visions, we can try to construct a fuller picture of what is implicit in the gospel sayings. We have already seen how so many of the characteristics of the Enochic Son of Man fit the gospel pictures.

In addition we have the vision in 2 Esdras 13 of a man coming from the sea before going to heaven on clouds. Is this a memory of some aspect of the ancient coronation ceremony in the autumn? We can only speculate. There was, for example, a great bronze sea in the temple of Solomon (1 Kings 7.23–26) which was half as wide as the temple itself (1 Kings 6.2; cf. 7.23). It was used for the priests to wash in (2 Chron. 4.6). Did the king also wash before his coronation? Did he emerge from the water and then enact the heavenly ascent and enthronement with the words of Psalm 2: 'You are my son, today I have begotten you'? This aspect of the Son of Man figure might then explain the story of the baptism of Jesus, which exists in two versions. The earliest Latin translation of the New Testament had a different account of the voice from heaven. It said: 'Thou art my son; today I have begotten thee,' rather than the more familiar, 'with thee I am well pleased'. In other words, there were some early Christians who associated the baptism of Jesus with the coronation of the ancient kings, and they believed that Jesus became fully the son of God at this time. This was the beginning of his kingship. Later, when Jesus the king entered Jerusalem, he was greeted with palms (Matt. 21.1–11). When he was lifted up on the cross he was recognized as king by Pilate (John 19.19–22) and as a Son of God by the centurion (Mark 15.39). When he was finally exalted he went with clouds (Acts 1.9). All this is royal imagery, the imagery of one 'like a son of man'.

We shall never know for certain how Jesus saw his role, but we must allow common sense to work alongside scholarship in this matter of what was meant by the phrase 'Son of Man'. We have to ask if the early Church could have attached the Danielic Son of Man figure to Jesus if this had not been a part of his teaching from the beginning. We have to ask if the Christian prophet who put the discourses of the Fourth Gospel into the mouth of Jesus would have been accepted as genuine if his words had not had the ring of truth. On balance, it seems that the

Son of Man in some form, together with the associated imagery and theology which we find in other Son of Man texts, does go back to Jesus himself in the Christian tradition. 'Associated imagery and theology' is an important part of the argument. If we restrict the Son of Man to Daniel 7, and assume (and it is only an assumption) that everyone else copied and altered this one source, we have very little to work on, and this is always fertile ground for scholarly ingenuity. By disallowing all the evidence it is possible to show that there is no evidence, and that the distinctive Son of Man theology was invented by the early Christians. But if we take seriously the whole intricate web of association, we see how deeply the Son of Man ideas were embedded in the Gospels. Not only do they appear in the Son of Man sayings, but also in passages which assume associated ideas such as the secret of the Messiah, or the intersection of human and divine in chosen angelic persons. It then becomes very difficult to be rid of the Son of Man. On the contrary, we have to make it a central theme, and use it as our best insight into the mind of Jesus.

Later generations ceased to use the designation because it was too deeply rooted in a particular setting and pattern of ideas. The title Christ eventually superseded all others, and Son of Man came to mean the earthly aspect of Jesus.

Can there be anything in this which is relevant to the world beyond that of first-century Palestine? Should we, like the second generation of Christians, use Son of Man to mean just a human being? If we do this we shall be true to much of later tradition, but we shall lose a valuable insight into Christian origins. There may be no direct relevance of writings like the Similitudes; Enoch's Son of Man figure is an angelic judge, a character more at home in the fantasy world of science fiction than the quiet respectability of the established Church. Equally it could be argued that there is no direct relevance of much of the New Testament. We have made it relevant by controlling it with our tradition and making it speak English. But the insights conveyed by the Son of Man traditions are as important as they ever were. The Son of Man judged the kings and the mighty, and they eventually recognized in a human figure, in one like themselves, the final claims of the justice of God. And one 'like a son of man', the human being who linked two creations, bringing heaven to earth and taking earthly things up into the vision of God, was the means of restoring the broken cosmic covenant and healing the wounds of a creation held prisoner to evil. Even today such a Son of Man has nowhere to lay his head.

Postscript

The evidence from Qumran shows that 1 Enoch was a pre-Christian text. The New Testament and the early Christian writers show that it was used by the first Christians. But where did it come from and who wrote it? Can we assume that because it was found at Qumran it was written there? We must put the same questions to this book as we put to the biblical books: 'Was it transmitted orally?'; Was it compiled from written sources?'; Has it been edited, altered, developed in the course of its history? And who preserved the tradition, compiled the work, revised the text and used its characteristic theology? I have mentioned already how scholars have a double standard when it comes to the dating of non-biblical texts; a book like 1 Enoch has been dated to the third century BC at the earliest because there are third-century BC manuscript remains. Nobody would date a biblical text by that method. When the fragments of 1 Enoch were found at Qumran, they had already had one lifetime; the texts had been used and copied by the community, but we do not know where they came from, or why that community considered them so important that they had several copies. We have to start with open minds, and ask when 1 Enoch might have been written, where the ideas originated, and who cherished them sufficiently to preserve and transmit them. We have to ask how these texts relate to the Old Testament, and not assume that they are a later, inferior work, dependent on the Old Testament.

Some parts of the work may have been transmitted orally, for example the Similitudes. These three parallel accounts of the last judgement are evidence of diversity within a tradition. One framework is common to each, but the details differ. The Enoch figure is not a part of the account, but only an observer of the heavenly events. Who could have composed and then preserved these elaborate texts? There are word patterns and recurring themes which suggest a period of oral transmission, but on what occasion might a vision of the judgement have been recounted? One method used to identify the setting of biblical material is 'form criticism'. The type of a text is established by comparing it with similar material, and thus a possible

THE LOST PROPHET

setting and function for it can be suggested. When we find something which has no obvious parallel in the Old Testament, we have to work in the dark. We simply do not know the setting for materials such as this, and if we do not know the setting we cannot be certain about their age. The imagery in the Similitudes is that of a royal cult; perhaps they were memories of the great ceremonial of the first temple. If so, it would have been devotees of that temple who preserved them. The only clear reference to a similar tradition in the biblical texts is Daniel 7, but much of that vision too is still obscure to us. What we have is a heavenly vision which is interpreted and applied to the people of 'Daniel's' time. It was interpreted, and this is the important thing to remember. Something older was being re-used. There is much of Daniel we still do not understand, especially the passages which deal with the angel figures and the temple setting (e.g. Dan. 8.11–12). Everything similar to Daniel 7 in later tradition is often thought to be derived from it, because the material in the vision is generally assumed to have been original to Daniel, or to have had pagan antecedents and therefore no possible roots in older biblical texts. We can no longer be so sure. It is more likely that Daniel had its roots in the lost tradition preserved only in 1 Enoch and related texts.

Who was preserving these ancient ideas about the angels and the temple? The Qumran community were certainly very interested in both; that is why they had books like 1 Enoch. We know from their own compositions that they had had disagreements with the Jerusalem temple, both its practices and its priests. But if they were not the original compilers of 1 Enoch, we have to look for another, earlier group. Had there once been people with temple interests (i.e. priests), who considered themselves purists and preservers of ancient ways, and who found themselves separated from the Jerusalem temple, perhaps expelled? The Enochic version of the history of the return from Babylon certainly makes it clear that the returned exiles were innovators whose ways were not acceptable. By implication, the Enoch group preserved older ways. Now religious groups who separate themselves in opposition to change and reform may themselves change and develop; but they may also preserve elements of the earliest ways which were the original cause of the separation. It is a situation such as this that we have to envisage as the origin for the vivid accounts of the judgement in the Similitudes. Details may have been added over the centuries, because the texts were in constant use. The essential framework, however, was very old.

At one stage, the Enoch figure was identified with the Son of Man, the agent of the divine judgement. Just the same process is visible in the Book of the Watchers: the myth of the fallen angels was offered as the background to the call of Enoch; he had to deliver the message of judgement. These two examples (there are more) show that 1 Enoch re-used earlier materials which had not previously been associated exclusively with Enoch, because they make perfect sense without him. The account of the origin of evil, and the account of its end, do not depend on Enoch, even though he is made the messenger and agent of judgement. Enoch was commissioned in the manner of the ancient prophets. If the myths of 1 Enoch are ancient, perhaps those prophets were commissioned in a similar setting?

The Book of the Watchers is also a composite work. Two versions of the angel myth are interwoven, just as different versions of ancient tales are combined in the early chapters of Genesis. If we can now see two interwoven stories, we may assume that these stories once existed separately. One described the fall of Asael to teach the heavenly wisdom on earth, the other the fall of two hundred angels who lusted after earthly wives and fathered demon offspring. When the Genesis writer used the ancient myths, he combined them with a theological purpose. The ancient stories were used to make a point relevant to the concerns of the compiler. The process was not simply one of collecting old tales in an approximately chronological order. The compiler of the Book of the Watchers worked in a similar way. The two tales as we now read them make the angel marriages the first sin, and the corruption of wisdom a consequence of this. 'Enoch' announces judgement. It is widely thought that this section is a comment upon the impurities and corruptions of the second temple priesthood, who thought of the priestly role as angelic, enacting on earth the role of the angels in the heavenly temple. If this is so, then the ancient compiler was working in a similar way to the compiler of Genesis. When would such a comment have been apt? Here again we have to guess. Other comments in 1 Enoch suggest that the crucial division occurred after the return of the exiles from Babylon. Their cult, and presumably their priests too, were neither pure nor acceptable.

The Apocalypse of Weeks is evidence that the Enochic tradition not only had ancient texts but also expounded them in the light of current concerns. The Aramaic text differs from the Ethiopic at this point. The older version shows that the 'weeks' were once a sequence of ten, not an interrupted sequence as in the Ethiopic. Most significant is the way in which a key verse (1 Enoch 91.11) has been expanded in the manner of a Targum (a commentary), in order to emphasize what was intended by 'the roots of violence' and 'the structure of falsehood'. We have here an older text made relevant to the Maccabean crisis.

All this is, and must remain, speculation. What I am suggesting raises many problems. It implies that the Judaism of the second temple period was more complex and varied than we had imagined. There were other heirs to ancient Israel than the Jews and the Samaritans. Not all of them had the same traditions and the same books. We hear, for example, very little of the holy books of the Samaritans, some of which were different from those of the Old Testament, and we concentrate exclusively on those of the Jews which became the Old Testament. The fact that we know nothing of the history of the Enoch writings shows us only how little we know, not that the Enoch writings had no history. Once we have begun this sort of speculation, many other possibilities present themselves. If the ideas in 1 Enoch are very old, this explains why so much of it is different from the Old Testament. The parts which do resemble the Old Testament (the Similitudes, for example, are very similar in parts to Isa. 24–7) are not necessarily derived from the Old Testament. They could equally be ancient accounts of the same ideas. It has generally been assumed that because 1 Enoch has 'used' parts of the Old Testament, it must have been a later and therefore an inferior text. It 'added' to the tradition which was preserved in a pure form only in the canonical texts. We now have to consider very carefully an exactly opposite position, that 1 Enoch preserves ancient ideas that have dropped from the Old Testament.

Had 1 Enoch been composed during the troubles of the second century BC, it would have been interesting, but not really very important, to discover that the early Christians used it. But if, as seems possible, it was an ancient text which preserved memories of the cult of the first temple and of the role of the anointed kings, the Messiahs, then it is very significant indeed that this book and its symbolism were used by the first Christians. It would mean, for example, that the division implied in 1 Enoch between those who kept to the old ways and those who returned from Babylon with Ezra in order to re-establish Jerusalem was the real root of the division we find in the New Testament. Ezra was associated with the Law; the Enochic group kept the ancient Messianic ideal, and had no place for Moses.

We have then to ask who or what Jesus thought he was. If he and his followers lived in the world of 1 Enoch, it explains many of the developments of early Christology, beliefs about the nature of the Messiah. It also brings into question many of the tendencies of New Testament scholarship which attribute all the 'mythology' of Christianity to later additions, and deny that Jesus saw himself in that way. Compare these two extracts. The first is from someone who questions the idea that most Christian theology grew up in addition to the ideas of Jesus himself:

> the 'apotheosis of the crucified Jesus' must already have taken place in the forties, and one is tempted to say that more happened in this period of less than two decades than in the whole of the next seven centuries, up to the time when the doctrine of the early church was completed. Indeed, one might even ask whether the formation of doctrine in the early church was essentially more than a consistent development and completion of what had already been unfolded in the primal event of the first two decades, but in the language and thought-forms of Greek, which was its necessary setting. (M. Hengel, *The Son of God*, London, SCM Press 1976, p.2)

The second is from someone who sees emphasis upon the ordinariness of Jesus as the basis for a new understanding between Jews and Christians:

> Anyone who starts with the historical human being, Jesus of Nazareth, and seeks to understand him in the Jewish milieu of his time, will recognise later Christological developments as mythological. These myths can contain deep insight about the meaning and significance of Jesus, but taken literally, they make Jesus the object of worship instead of the Father. (M. Braybrooke, 'When Jesus was a Jew', *The Guardian*, 23 November 1987)

Both cannot be true. There is no doubt that Christianity *did* develop once it was transplanted into a Greek setting, but to what extent? Was it the essential insight that altered, or only the way in which it was expressed?

It is becoming more and more difficult to speak with confidence about the religious scene in Jesus' time. Many attempts have been made to reconstruct it. Initially this was done without any real use of contemporary Jewish materials, and the resulting picture was necessarily distorted. The next stage was to use 'Jewish' materials, but many of these were from a period two or three centuries after the time of Jesus. The written evidence from this later period was projected back into New Testament times, and was also giving a far from accurate picture. We used to speak of Orthodox Judaism at a period when such a thing did not exist. The great catastrophe of AD 70, when the Romans destroyed Jerusalem, led to a restructuring of Judaism in order to survive in the new situation. What happened after AD 70 cannot be used as background to the life of Jesus. We have a circular argument. Later 'Jewish' materials were used to reconstruct what Jesus must have been like; it is hardly surprising that he was found to be an ordinary Jew of his time. The more colourful aspects of New Testament theology were thus confirmed as later additions, possibly from well-intentioned pagan converts who brought their paganism with them into their new faith. This contribution from Jewish scholars is to be welcomed, but we cannot expect them to have an entirely unbiased approach.

The texts found at Qumran are helping us to see that the religious scene in Palestine was more complex and varied than anything which could have been constructed from later Jewish materials. We are discovering evidence for beliefs and ways of interpreting Scripture which give us a much fuller picture of what happened. But still we know too little for certainty. What we must do is recognize that our former certainties were ill-founded, and be prepared for the unsettling process of launching out towards a new understanding of Jesus and the early Christian writings. This new understanding need not be destructive if it is broadly based. We must not replace one distortion with another. If we take a broad basis for our reconstruction, and include the Enochic writings, we reach a very different conclusion about the nature of Jesus and the period in which Christian theology developed. 1 Enoch was abandoned by Jewish tradition very early; it survived only as a 'Christian' book, even though it was pre-Christian. In the early Christian centuries Jews regarded the Enoch figure with distaste. The pictures of Jesus based only on 'Jewish' materials conclude that all the 'supernatural' ideas in later Christology were added by followers, but this is because these 'Jewish' reconstructions do not use the Enochic material which we know was a part of the first Christians' world. Thus they are able to reach their conclusions about Jesus as the faithful Jew of his time, turned into something else by his followers.

What might someone whose mental framework included 1 Enoch have thought about Jesus? Indeed, what did Jesus think about himself? One of the keys to this, as I said in chapter 7, is the designation 'son of man'. If Jesus used it of himself, and used it in the Enochic way, then there was little of the 'mythological' development of Christianity which did not originate with Jesus himself. His references to the great judgement, the healing miracles and the exorcisms all point this way. What we should love to know is more about Jesus' own self-awareness, his own inner life. What exactly were the encounters with Satan which are described in Matthew 4 and Luke 4? A visionary experience of all the kingdoms of the world in a moment of time was certainly not out of place in the world of Enoch. (Enoch had a similar experience, 1 Enoch 87.3. From a high place he saw history unfold before him.) Nor are the expelled demons and the vision of Satan falling from heaven out of character (Luke 10.18).

What happens to our picture of Jesus, and to our picture of Christianity, if we bring back the insights and ideas of 1 Enoch? Or, we might say, how would Christianity have been different if 1 Enoch had stayed in favour, and not been condemned and dropped by the Western Churches? We should have a Messiah figure, a son of man, who was the intermediary between heaven and earth, a figure who functioned in both worlds. He was a priest who interceded in the heavenly temple. On earth he was the messenger who announced the great judgement, and in heaven he was the agent of that judgement. He was the centre of the great cosmic covenant which kept the creation in its appointed order. He was the bastion against the forces of evil which threatened the people of God, and the order of creation. His was the name which could bind the unruly forces of evil, and expel the demons which infested the earth. He was the source of righteousness, by which was meant wholeness, healing and restoration for the victims of evil. The reign of this son of man was a time when nature was restored to fertility, and humankind to peace.

Much of this is already a part of the traditional picture of Jesus; it is the very part usually attributed to later pagan developments. The parts which are new (e.g. the cosmic covenant), are those not mentioned specifically in the New Testament, but only implied in passages such as Romans 8. Some parts of the Enochic picture are quite clear in the New Testament, but have received little emphasis. These include its belief about the origin of evil. The New Testament provides ample evidence for belief in external forces of evil which corrupt and destroy both the creation and human lives, but this has been overshadowed by an overwhelming emphasis upon individual sin, and the burden of human guilt. Wounds have been inflicted, when the original intention was to heal and to restore an already afflicted creation. The story of Adam and Eve, and the sin of Eve, have no part in this scheme.

The most important feature of the Enochic theology is its emphasis upon the nature and the role of knowledge. All knowledge of the creation comes from God; used apart from God, it destroys everything. The myths in Enoch describe vividly what we should call technology, the production of weapons, communication, the formation of expectations and opinions, medicine, politics and even the world of fashion (bracelets, ornaments, the use of antimony and the beautifying of the eyelids, 1 Enoch 8.1), and what happens when these are used in rebellion against God. The possession of such knowledge or wisdom eventually transforms a human being into a son of God; but the sons of God were those who fell and thought that they were entitled to rule the earth themselves. Many of these ideas about the role of knowledge resemble those of the later Gnostics, whose developed thought was condemned by the Church as heresy. We have kept the belief that we are sons of God as the result of baptism; we rarely emphasize what this actually means.

The most important implication of the Enochic theology concerns the nature of Israel's religion before the exile. The complex beliefs about divine beings, and the role of the king as one of those divine beings, one who was both mortal and a member of the heavenly court, must be relevant to our understanding of the divine nature of Jesus. The pre-exilic religion of Israel was not monotheistic. There were many divine beings of various ranks, and the king was believed to be one of them, the visible representative and representation of God on earth, his son. We find hints of this in many places in the Old Testament (e.g. 1 Chron. 29.23; Ps. 2; the Greek of Ps. 110.3, which says: 'I have begotten you' not 'your youth'). If we could penetrate further into the lost world which we glimpse in 1 Enoch, we should be able to understand what the earliest Christians meant when they called Jesus 'Son of God' and 'Son of Man'.

1 Enoch represents the written deposit of these ideas; many of them, perhaps most of them, were transmitted in a more diffuse way; the old ways were breathed in with the air. There was probably no conscious transmission of many of these beliefs about angels and their roles. The beliefs were just there. They penetrated every aspect of life. They were used to explain the weird landscape of the Dead Sea valley,

the problems with the calendar, the manic policies of Antiochus Epiphanes, disease, and so on. And it is because they were just there, a part of the accepted view of the world, that these beliefs are not spelt out as a separate issue in the New Testament. Many of its passages make a great deal of sense if read in the light of these beliefs; but there is no way that we can expect the New Testament texts to give us an exact authentication of every aspect of this world-view. It is this uncertainty which is unsettling, because the new light on some areas is very dramatic, and shows us how much we have lost. If we do not use it we shall lose a most exciting opportunity to increase our knowledge of early Christianity.

Index